THE TEAM TH[illegible]DREAM

The amazing ris[illegible]

from Division Three to [illegible]EFA Cup

Jon Tait © Copyright 2007

All rights reserved

No parts of this publication may be reproduced, stored in a retrieval system, or transmitted in any form or by any means, electronic, mechanical, photocopying, recording or otherwise without the prior permission of the copyright owner.

British Library Cataloguing In Publication Data
A Record of this Publication is available
from the British Library

ISBN 978-1-84685-594-8

First Published 2007 by
Exposure Publishing,
an imprint of
Diggory Press Ltd
Three Rivers, Minions, Liskeard, Cornwall, PL14 5LE, UK
and of Diggory Press, Inc.,
Goodyear, Arizona, USA
WWW.DIGGORYPRESS.COM

To Sally

One

Season 02/03

Back into Scotland

ROWAN ALEXANDER was a strike partner of Frank McAvennie at St. Mirren and played against Johan Cruyff and a young Ruud Gullit at Feyenoord in the UEFA Cup during his playing career. While McAvennie had a reputation as a glamour boy during the Eighties with his bleached blonde long hair and Champagne lifestyle, Alexander was hard-working, dogged and focused, not afraid to get stuck in and these were the characteristics that he would take with him into management.

Rowan's playing career started out at Queen of the South where he netted 69 goals in 136 League games for the Doonhamers. He moved on to St. Mirren and then Brentford and became a terrace legend at Greenock Morton where his goals helped fire the Cappielow side to the First Division Championship. Rowan spent nine seasons at Morton, hitting 87 goals in 310 League games.

"I played for Frank McLintock's Brentford and scored a minute into my debut in the Milk Cup against Gary Lineker's Leicester. I scored again two minutes later but was given offside. However, I came back to Scotland and St. Mirren and played up front with McAvennie. But then I got put into midfield and that is when Saints played Feyenoord in the UEFA Cup in 1983/84 and I was up against Cruyff and Gullit. It was an incredible experience."

He moved into management at Queen of the South in 1996 before taking charge at Raydale in the Unibond League in November 2000.

"Gretna were bottom of the league of 24 teams when I took over and we finished 17th. It was never our intention to play in the re-structured Conference North and South Leagues due to the travel and financial costs. I had a five-year plan and knew as soon as I stepped in the door that we could do it," said Alexander.

His burning ambition was to get the club into the SFL and himself and then-assistant Derek Frye hand-delivered videos and pamphlets outlining the club's history and plans to every one of the league's teams when the vacancy arose with the demise of Airdrionans in 2002.

And it proved third time lucky for Gretna as their successful election to the Scottish Football League at Hampden Park in June 2002 followed two failed attempts from the club in 1994 and 1999.

Concerns over the precedent which would be set by allowing a proposed new club, Airdrie United, to simply replace liquidated Airdrieonians, ultimately influenced the vote in Gretna's favour.

The five other clubs applying for the vacancy - Gala Fairydean, Cove Rangers, Huntly, Edinburgh City and Preston Athletic - were never in the hunt as it came down to straight choice between Gretna and Airdrie United.

Gretna won the first ballot, but without achieving the necessary 14 votes of the 27 cast by the SFL chairmen who had listened to ten-minute presentations by each applicant. In the second ballot, Gretna triumphed by 16 votes to Airdrie United's 11.

"The chairmen of all the teams were in a big room and we were invited to sit at the back for the result. The first person I saw was Douglas Rae from my old club Morton and he winked at me. I knew then we were in and I went to the back of the room and just burst into tears," said Rowan.

"When I came to Gretna, getting into the Scottish League was one of my main aims so it was a fabulous day for us," he said.

"I think the major factor in our success was that our house is in order, we are financially sound and have a structure more than capable of sustaining itself in the SFL."

"I think people were worried about the implications of letting Airdrie in, in terms of other clubs doing the same if they went bust, and it swayed the vote for us."

Airdrie United did get into the SFL as well, however, as they stepped up to replace Clydebank.

Gretna Football Club's formation in 1946 had much to do with John 'Jock' Kerr who was playing for Solway Star when his brother, who worked at the dog track at Albion Rovers Cliftonhill stadium, tipped off Queen's Park who were impressed with what they saw and signed him up.

He worked as a fitter in the shipyards while at the Spiders and went on to play professionally at Blackburn Rovers and Brentford.

While at Brentford he played alongside Patsy Hendren, one of only a handful of men to have played internationally at both football and cricket.

But his playing career was finished when he damaged his cruciate ligament playing against Charlton Athletic at the Valley and he returned home to Gretna.

Jock was a driving force behind the early Gretna Football Club.

"There had been a few teams in Gretna but until this club was formed someone always ran away with the money and the clubs folded after a season or so," said Tom Kerr, honorary life President of Gretna FC and son of Jock.

The McKinnel family was only too happy to help out in an advisory capacity as when Jock Kerr had been playing at Ewood Park, the McKinnel's father had gone to Blackburn for trials and had formed a lasting friendship with him.

"Everybody in Gretna was behind it. We were allowed to change in the school and walked up to Station Park. We took the goalposts up with us, and they had to be taken down after every game as a condition of us getting the field," said Tom, who played for Cliftonville in Belfast with five Northern Irish internationals during the War before coming home to play in Gretna's inaugural team.

The first season was played in the Dumfries Junior League at Station Park on Mackie's field. The players had to supply their own white shirt and their black shorts were made by Mrs. J. Kerr, who had been a dressmaker.

The team was started so the people of Gretna could say, on returning from the forces, we have a football club and a social club.

The following people, all from Gretna, gave £10 to get the club started up. Mr. Liddle (School master), G. Glasspool (Teacher), A. Thorburn (Dentist), M.Todd (Baker), J. Kerr (Shop), H. McMahone, J. Mitchell (Chemist), T. Kerr and W. Kerr (Just de-mobbed after the War). £10 was a week's wages in 1946.

The money from a national sweep was used to buy Raydale Park. During the First World War Raydale was the site of a hospital and the ground belonged to them. The ground cost around £400.

"Mrs. Fisher the schoolteacher formed an entertainments committee and we had dance nights in the Crown and Mitre in Carlisle and up at Eastriggs," said Tom Kerr.

The club also ran a sports day and 5-a-side competition in 1951 in which the legendary Bill Shankly entered a team. His brother also came down from Falkirk along with Ayr United, Kilmarnock, Queen of the South, Queen's Park, St. Cuthbert Wanderers and Newton Stewart.

"One of the Shankly games was locked at 0-0 and Bill shouted 'Do you want me to come on the park and put it in for you,'" said Tom, who got friendly with the great man over the years.

Shankly had called Tom up for Carlisle United to play against Spennymoor before the War.

"In that season we played Penrith three times in front of crowds of three to five thousand," said David Scott, who also played in Gretna's first team.

"It was just after the War and football was picking up again. Attendances were good," he explained.

"That many lads who came home from War played or watched. When you were in the forces you played for your unit and they were continuing that," said Tom Kerr.

"Jock Kerr probably had the most say in picking the team as he was so well known. People knew he had played at Queen's Park and these places," said Tom Kerr.

David Scott added: "There was no official manager, it was run by the committee. Jock would have the most football knowledge. He could tell by the way people ran whether they would be a player or not."

Football Club meetings were held in the sorting room of Gretna Post Office. The club had moved South into England and the Carlisle & District League after one season.

"The Carlisle League had been going for years and was more experienced than the one on the other side of the Border. There was a better standard of football and the travelling was shorter," said Tom.

"When Raydale Park was purchased there was still much work to do on the ground, and many people came to the club's rescue," said Tom.

"Jack Bowes, who was the Bowling Green greenkeeper, advised. Hughie Marshall did a lot of work on the ground and Hugh McMahone practically lived there. Fred Irvine cut the grass when required and George Hardistry helped with transport. Many people in Gretna came along and gave a helping hand. Until the field and stand were completed, Mr. J. Mitchell kindly allowed all meetings to take place on his premises, the sorting office. Numerous jobs needed to be done, but fortunately there was always local people that helped out. We had tremendous support from the local people, too numerous to mention, and when Gretna played Penrith away a special train ran from Gretna Green along with the player's bus and two bus loads of supporters. These were marvellous days," said Tom.

When the membership of the football club was growing they decided to get an alcohol licence but were refused as licensing control would not allow it on the same site as the football ground.

The committee progressed and built the social club, real name 'The Gretna Social & Athletic Club' as the word football was not allowed because of the aforementioned laws.

"When the committee was formed Ian Dalgliesh was about 15 years old, and with talking with Mr. Todd, where he learned his trade in Todd's Baker shop, became an enthusiastic lover of the club which in later years led to various roles on the committee and along with Tom Kerr and Tom Straitton saw the club evolve from its early days to its acceptance in the Scottish League," said John Kerr, son of Tom.

Tom Kerr was a wireless operator in the RAF during the War and played for Cliftonville while in Belfast for three years.

He spent almost another three years abroad in India, Indo-China and Saigon, where he caught malaria twice.

"One of the most embarrassing things was when I was based in Belfast and had to go down to Dublin to relieve wireless operators in the South. When Cliftonville played Dublin teams in pre-season I had to pretend I didn't know Dublin. We had to go down in used civilian clothes as we couldn't go down in uniform," smiled Tom, his white hair still combed immaculately and sat in a grey suit.

He continued playing and worked on the mail train when he came home in the Gretna team which lined up: Mitchell, Barry, Wallace, B. Kerr, Bryson, Robinson, Scott, T. Kerr, B. Routledge, K. White, C. Earsman.

"Tommy MacFarlane's trick was to stand with the centre half marking him and he'd just pull his shirt to get in front of him and he was away," said Tom.

"He was sent off one week and the opponent complained – 'he's just a street corner boy!'" he said.

"Walter Barry was very professional and when he tackled he hit the ball and the man so you couldn't really call it a foul. He was good in the air and played for Queens Park Rangers. He was getting on in years when he played for us but he was probably one of the best we had. He was a good man to have on your side – you wouldn't want to play against him," said Tom.

"The players all got on together and there were never any problems with the players. We all looked after each other," said David Scott.

"Someone was roughing me up one game and Ken White said to him 'Do that again and you'll have me to answer to.' I came down from Alloa many years ago and it will be great to see them at Raydale. It is tremendous progress from a team just starting up to where they are now."

Amongst the club's best known players of this successful era were Billy Cross who skippered the team for several years without missing a match, and strikers Dennis 'Touchy' Smith and the late Tommy McFarlane, who each hold the distinction of scoring over 100 goals in a season. Six consecutive Carlisle and District League titles proved that the club was becoming too strong for its local surroundings and the club was admitted to the newly formed Second Division of the Northern League in 1982, spending over £100,000 on upgrading the ground to the standards required by the League.

Promotion to the First Division was achieved at the first attempt and the club spent nine successful seasons at this level culminating in back-to-back championships in 1990-91 and 1991-92, the latter ensuring promotion to the First Division of the Northern Premier (UniBond) League.

In 1999 Gretna beat Glasgow Rangers 2-1 in a match arranged to raise money for the Lockerbie Air Disaster. In their first season in the UniBond the club finished sixth and reached the semi-final of the League Cup.

Although the team was not able to match that League position again in the Nineties they hit national headlines by reaching the 1st round of the F. A. Cup where they acquitted themselves well v Rochdale (1991-92) and Bolton Wanderers (1993-94).

"We did worry that playing in English football for so long would be an obstruction for us," said Alexander, "especially in view of the Old Firm's attempts to move to England, but we are a Scottish club and we wanted to play in Scotland."

And so a part-time team of joiners, builders, electricians and young skill seekers pulled on the black and white shirt for Gretna's historic first game in the SFL which was marked by a bumper full-house crowd for the poignant visit of Morton, where Rowan Alexander's goalscoring exploits had made him a hero, and the teams were piped out onto the pitch.

Gretna were in no way overawed by the occasion and took just 19 seconds to mark their entry into the Scottish Third Division.

Matt Henney collected a poor goal-kick from Morton keeper Craig Coyle before firing low into the net to give them a dream start.

But the visitors responded and a couple of crosses caused goalkeeper David Mathieson trouble before wing-back Derek

Collins' ball was bundled into the net by Warren Hawke for the leveller.

The second half failed to reach the heights of the opening period, the game becoming littered with fouls, and neither team could string passes together.

The late introduction of player-boss Alexander sparked new life into the game, although the few chances created by both teams were off target.

Brooks Mileson had been at the game with a Northern League delegation. Self-made millionaire, visionary and football fanatic Brooks was born in the tough Pennywell area of Sunderland and started his working life in accountancy before transferring to the building industry. In 1981 the Southern contractor with whom he was employed closed the Northern Company. So he started his own £100 limited Construction Company as there were very few job opportunities in the Northeast at the time. He became involved in the Insurance industry with a four-branch insurance intermediary and built this up to one of the largest intermediary chains in the UK before selling out to Budget Insurance.

On the back of the client base he built up the Albany Claims Group which included claims management, non-fault car hire and legal medical reporting to the largest independent claims management group before selling to Help Hire PLC in 2004.

He still has business interests in construction, team wear, an American software security house and a UK security company.

Brooks broke his back aged eleven in a quarry accident and was told that he would never walk again. He taught himself to walk. He was then told that he would never be able to take part in sport as the accident also damaged his right kidney, now removed, and affected his hips and right leg. He wore built-up shoes in an attempt to realign and ran for England in the 1967 International Cross Country Championships, gaining an individual bronze and team gold. He was a four-minute miler, even though he hated running. Brooks didn't start smoking until his fifties, but soon built up a 100-a-day Marlboro habit. He was, in short, a man who didn't do things by half.

Wearing jeans and with his hair in a ponytail and sporting a goatee beard, Brooks shunned the boardroom in favour of standing with the fans on the terraces.

He met the manager and was impressed with what Rowan had to say, agreeing to sponsor the club's youth programme.

In mid-week Gretna went out of the Bell's Scottish League Challenge Cup first round after a 2-1 defeat at Queen's Park. It was tiny Gretna's first ever visit to Hampden Park and was marked with a presentation before the game from their Glasgow hosts.

Gretna started better with chances falling to Mark Dobie and John Hore in the opening 10 minutes.

But Queen's went in front with their first attempt on goal when young striker Steven Canning did well under pressure to head the ball into the top corner from six yards.

However, the introduction of two substitutes early in the second half, one of them being manager Rowan Alexander, boosted Gretna.

And the equaliser soon came when Dobie went past two defenders to calmly slot the ball home.

Then, with eight minutes remaining, Queens Park hit the winner when John Gemmill scored with another header from six yards out.

Gretna secured their first victory in Scottish League football on the Saturday thanks to first-half goals from Mark Dobie and Steve Skinner in a 2-0 success at Elgin City.

Dobie opened the scoring in the 13th minute with a clinical finish after Skinner capitalised on some slack Elgin defending.

Gretna doubled their lead in the 31st minute when Dobie returned the compliment and Skinner curled home past stranded goalkeeper Martin Pirie.

It could have been much worse for the home side had it not been for Pirie, who performed heroics in the Elgin goal as Gretna sealed an impressive win.

New boys Gretna then proved they were a force to be reckoned with after an emphatic 4-1 win over Montrose.

They were in control for most of the game, although Montrose dominated the opening stages and their early efforts were rewarded after just seven minutes when some sloppy defending led to a goal for Chris Webster. But Gretna kept pushing and levelled in the 25th minute when Davie Irons powered the ball into the net.

Gretna went in front before half-time when Mark Dobie found himself in front of goal with just the goalkeeper to beat and he made no mistake.

The second half saw Gretna continue to dominate despite the Gable Endies best efforts. They went 3-1 up after 62 minutes through a John Hore strike and 20 minutes later Hore struck again.

And Gretna stunned the SFL as they moved to the top of the Third Division following a 2-0 win against Albion Rovers at Raydale.

The Borderers missed a host of opportunities in the first half but made the breakthrough midway through the second period as a mix-up in the Albion defence left Ryan McGuffie with just the goalkeeper to beat and he powered the ball into the top-left corner.

They continued to push forward and sealed victory in the 82nd minute when John Hore slotted home.

But Queen's Park skipper Danny Ferry then scored the only goal of the game at Hampden as Gretna went down 1-0. Ferry pounced on a loose ball in midfield in the 14th minute and powered his way forward, playing a neat one-two with John Gemmell before coolly slotting the ball home.

Queen's almost added a second just seven minutes later, with goalkeeper David Matheson palming James Allan's shot over the crossbar.

But Gretna also had their chances and veteran midfielder David Irons came closest to saving the game for them with a fierce shot from distance.

Keeper Colin Stewart, on loan from Kilmarnock, denied Irons again at the death with a good diving save.

Irons did find the net in the CIS Cup at home to East Fife, but Gretna went out 2-1 and they then collapsed to their second defeat of the league campaign as they were ruthlessly dismantled 4-1 by a rampant Peterhead at Raydale.

Rowan Alexander's side of league new boys were sitting second top of the table when they went into the game, but they were taught a harsh lesson by Ian Wilson's outfit.

Gretna were in trouble as early as the third minute when Kevin Tindal put the visitors ahead, but Alex Benjamin levelled three minutes after the break with a fine effort.

However, Peterhead were smack in form and they weren't leaving Gretna without all three points. They remained in a positive mood and grabbed a second through Andy Robbie in the 54th minute.

The game was wrapped up near the end when the Highlanders hit two in the space of six minutes. Roddie was on target again in the 78th minute and Lamile Camara added the fourth shortly afterwards.

Gretna took three gift-wrapped points away from Firs Park courtesy of some blundering home defending in a 4-0 success at East Stirling.

Alex Benjamin scored twice, with Matthew Henney and Steve Skinner grabbing one apiece as Gretna bounced back from the previous weekend's hammering.

A relatively even encounter was turned on its head three minutes short of the hour mark when East Stirlingshire's Bill Struthers left aback pass short with Mark Dobie shooting straight at keeper Scott Findlay with Henney firing in the rebound.

Dobie ran through a poorly organised offside trap two minutes later. His shot was again saved, but Benjamin was on hand to tap in the loose ball.

Substitute Skinner was allowed the freedom of the home penalty box to strike Gretna's third after 76 minutes.

Another disastrous piece of defending from Craig Reid with eight minutes remaining allowed Benjamin to collect the ball, round the goalkeeper, and stroke the ball into the empty net.

But boss Rowan Alexander blew his top and said his players didn't deserve to be paid after slumping to their third straight home defeat 2-0 against struggling Stirling Albion.

He said: "I'm disgusted and embarrassed by the players' attitude and the whole performance. They don't deserve to pick up their money after that. Right through the team - with the exception of Davie Irons and David Hewson - it was disgraceful. You'd think we were the team sitting at the bottom of the table. The players need to go home and take a good look at themselves. I've kids of 18 at the club with more determination and fighting spirit. The performance was totally unacceptable."

Colin McKinnon fired Albion in front after 15 minutes, meeting a deep cross from Robert Dunn with a glancing header that David Mathieson got a hand to but couldn't keep out.

Alex Benjamin fluffed a great chance to equalise in the 24th minute. Stirling's defence were playing statues when Ryan McGuffie's ball over the top sent him one-on-one with Chris Reid but he shot tamely and the keeper blocked the ball with his legs.

Adam Thwaites rescued Gretna with a goal-line clearance when McKinnon's header from a corner fell for Stevie Mallan to fire in a fierce ten-yarder.

But two minutes later Thwaites was daydreaming and played Nicholas on-side as Mallan threaded a ball through to him on the corner of the box.

Mathieson was unsighted as the ex-Motherwell starlet cut inside and lashed a low 15-yard shot through a defenders legs and wide of the keeper for number two.

In the second half Stirling were under siege but former Celtic defender Mark McNally marshalled Stirling's back line to snuff out Gretna's frontmen.

A James Graham hat-trick kept East Fife in the title chase after they came from behind to beat Gretna 3-2 the following week.

Matt Henney and John Hore had twice put Gretna in front before the Methill side hit back to ensure a return to the top of Division Three.

Gretna opened the scoring in the fourth minute when Mark Dobie's shot was tipped on to the post and Henney netted the rebound.

Graham equalised eight minutes later after goalkeeper David Mathieson spilled a cross.

But the Borderers regained the lead when Hore headed in Dobie's cross.

A controversial penalty, given when Mathieson was adjudged to have brought down Graham in the 52nd minute, gave the striker his second.

His treble arrived in the 70th minute, when he slammed in the rebound after Kenny Deuchar's shot was saved.

Rowan then warned his shot-shy strikers that he was ready to take their place after a 0-0 draw at home to Elgin. The 41-year old former Morton star was fed up watching his frontmen fire blanks and reckoned it was time to pull on the boots again.

"The strikers had no cutting edge and were guilty of poor finishing," he said. "It's something I'll have to address. It's possible the boots may have to come out of the locker again." In a first half plagued by offside decisions, City keeper Martin Pirie saved comfortably from Steve Skinner and had his palms stung by a Matt Henney 20-yarder.

He was finally beaten by a clever Adam Thwaites lob after the break but David MacKay raced back to clear off the line. For all Gretna's chances, Elgin almost won it with 15 minutes to play when Michael Teasdale nodded a deep cross back into the danger area and David Ross' powerful header rattled the crossbar.

Kyle May and Simon Eeles hit the net in a superb battling 2-2 draw at Morton and Gretna also took a point from bogey side Queen's Park - but had to wait until the last minute for the crucial equaliser at Raydale.

Queen's Park opened the scoring after 13 minutes when Steven Moffat scored from the penalty spot after Spiders striker James Allan was brought down in the box by Davie Irons.

But Gretna started pushing forward and had a number of chances. They equalised in the 34th minute when a Tommy Turner free kick ended up at the feet of Simon Eeles and he slotted it across the goalmouth and past Stewart.

Queen's Park took control at the start of the second half and began to create chances. They went 2-1 up after 69 minutes when substitute Patrick Gallagher swept a goalmouth fumble into the net after a corner.

But Gretna equalised just before the final whistle from a hotly-contested penalty. Mark Dobie fired the ball into the back of the net to share the points.

Ryan McGuffie hit the net in a 2-1 defeat at Albion Rovers and Matt Henney scored in a 1-1 draw at Peterhead before East Stirling supersub Derek Ure netted a last-gasp leveller for basement boys 'Shire just seven minutes after coming off the bench in a 2-2 draw at Raydale Park.

Steve Skinner gave Gretna an early lead when he skipped past three men and curled in a great shot. And he added a second in just 12 minutes after a blunder by keeper Scott Findlay. Jordan Leishman pulled one back for Shire in the 79th minute to give them hope. Ure completed the comeback.

And an astonishing injury-time double snatched the points for Jim Moffat's table topping East Fife in a 3-2 win at Raydale the next weekend as they again blew a two-goal lead.

Paul Mortimer's deflected 20-yard free-kick looked to have snatched a point for the Methill men but Kenny Deuchar ensured the Fifers grabbed all three points by holding off three challenges to fire low into the net.

East Fife boss Moffat said: "We showed great belief to come back. It was a great finish and great drama for the fans."

Gretna looked on easy street when Mark Dobie fired a 47th minute opener from Matt Henney's cross and they doubled their lead two minutes later as Marc Cleeland fired through Jim Butter's legs.

A thunderous John Ovenstone strike grabbed a lifeline for East Fife before they staged the grandstand finish.

Gretna gaffer Rowan Alexander must have been wondering what he had to do to win after a second half double from Albion Rovers fired them to the top of the table.

The answer might have been sitting in the stand.

Midfield maestro Mick Galloway's Gretna debut was put on ice after the Borderers' application for international clearance was not gained in time because of FIFA regulations.

But the former Carlisle United star was set to appear as a trialist at Stirling the following week and he would put pen to paper on a two-and-a-half year contract when the transfer window re-opened on January 1st.

"It was a chance that came out of the blue really," said Galloway.

"I've kept in touch with Rowan Alexander and Derek Frye ever since I came on loan last year. I've got a lot of time for them and they did me a favour last year by taking me on loan and helping me get fit after my injury."

Assistant boss Frye said: "Micky Galloway is a good signing, without a doubt. He will spread passes around the park all day for us."

The watching Galloway will have been impressed by the way Gretna matched the title contenders in every department in the first half.

In the 14th minute the hard-working Matt Henney crossed from the right and Mark Dobie hooked in a volley that lacked power and keeper Scott Shearer saved.

Rovers' respite was short lived as just three minutes later Gretna went in front. Davie Irons' cross was touched back to Henney by Skinner and his 16-yard shot took a wicked deflection off Peter Cormack and looped into the net.

Gretna wasted possession from a 29th minute free kick in a promising position but as Rovers unleashed a three-on-one break at pace, the cool-headed Kyle May snuffed out the danger.

The Cliftonhill side threatened with the aerial menace of towering Jim Mercer and the clever ball skills of Chris Silvestro but failed to deliver as Gretna's back line held firm.

Right on half time, Rovers' John Bradford showed great control to pull down a long ball over the top by Cormack, but his low shot flashed just wide.

That displayed their intent and after a dressing room roasting from boss Peter Hetherston, they came out guns blazing after the break.

Gretna keeper Dave Mathieson made two brilliant saves to deny Charlie MacLean and sub Iain Diack but Silvestro drilled home the equaliser from 20 yards in the 62nd minute.

Milligan cleared a Mercer header off the line and Bradford slammed a shot against the woodwork before Mercer acrobatically scissor-volleyed low beyond Mathieson for the 75th minute winner.

Frye said afterwards: "It's the same story every week. We go a goal up and can't defend. I'm not blaming defenders, yet you're looking at the team and saying to yourself just carry the game to them, play into the channels and squeeze the game. The frustrating thing for Rowan and I is that the game is there to be enjoyed. I can get frustrated and I can get angry but I'd just like to see then turning a corner because I don't think they're a bad side."

This was shown as David Irons hit the only goal in a 1-0 success at Stirling Albion and Gretna claimed back-to-back away wins with a 2-0 victory at Montrose. They took the lead after just five minutes when a great run by Steven Skinner set up John Hore who scored from close range and they wrapped up the points when Gavin Skelton netted in injury time.

Rowan Alexander revealed a spying mission gave him the vital information to help sabotage Cove Ranger's cup mission as Gretna went through in the Tennent's third round with a 3-0 win.

Alexander was delighted after his side comfortably saw off the Highland League outfit with a Mark Dobie double and a John Hore strike.

And he was even happier after learning his side had landed another home tie against Clyde in the third round.

"We'd done our homework and the players we thought might hurt us didn't. We've put in the hard work and got a nice early goal that kicked us into gear. The lads did a professional job and it was just a case of finishing off the chances that we created. Cove always posed a threat but that's three clean sheets on the trot and the defensive is proving to be a brick wall at the moment. I'm just delighted to be in the third round of the Scottish Cup. Everyone wants to pull out a big name but hopefully we've just buried our home hoodoo."

There was a real element of needle to the tie with Gretna having pipped Cove in the bid to land the vacant place in the Scottish League during the summer.

But since that glory day, Alexander had been frustrated by his side's dodgy home form.

He had strengthened the side in mid-week by signing experienced midfielders Keith Knox and Mick Galloway and striker Brian Fairbairn.

Gretna totally dominated after the Highlanders after a squad of volunteers had cleared snow from the Raydale pitch to ensure the game got underway.

Their hard work was rewarded as early as the fifth minute when John Hore crossed low and evergreen striker Dobie launched himself into a diving header which bulleted into the net from close range.

In the 19th minute Gretna worked the ball neatly to tricky winger Stevie Skinner, whose shot on the turn flew over the bar and five minutes later Tommy Turner had to make a brilliant last-ditch sliding tackle to deny Cove's Michael Beattie as he bore down on goal.

On the half hour Skinner picked up the ball on the edge of his own box from a poor Cove corner and ran the length of the pitch, only to be denied a brilliant solo goal by a last-gasp block from Kevin Allan as he shaped to shoot.

Soon after Hore's angled shot was tipped onto the bar by keeper Coull and skidded over onto the roof of the net.

After the break Dobie unleashed a curling 25-yard effort that Coull saved brilliantly at full stretch.

But within two minutes the Gretna advantage was doubled.

McGinley fouled Marc Cleeland on the edge of the box and Gavin Skelton's fierce free kick crashed into the wall. Hore reacted quickest to latch onto the loose ball, nip past the diving Coull and fire into the net from a narrow angle.

Gretna killed off Cove's hopes with quarter of an hour left when Hore released Skinner, who poked the ball into the path of Dobie.

The striker's initial shot was blocked by the unlucky Coull but the ball ricocheted up and into the net off Dobie's chest.

Cove boss Kevin Walker said: "I'm a bit disappointed as I don't think we did ourselves justice. I thought 3-0 flattered Gretna a bit but they were everything we were expecting - big and strong and physical. But, if I'm being honest, Gretna deserved to go through and I can't really have any complaints."

Another double from veteran striker Mark Dobie then earned Gretna their first-ever win at Hampden Park in a 2-1 league success over Queen's Park.

But Gretna had to survive a late rally from the Spiders after Johnny Whelan pulled a goal back 11 minutes from time. Dobie netted his first in the 16th minute when goalkeeper Tony Mitchell dropped a corner at his feet and added the second from the penalty spot 10 minutes later after John Hore had been tripped by Richard Sinclair.

Gretna seemed to be cruising to a comfortable win until Whelan headed in a cross from Steve Moffat.

Dobie was spot-on again in a 1-1 home draw with Peterhead with sub Keith Robertson keeping the Blue Toon's promotion push on track with a late leveller.

Robertson raced onto a Kevin Bissett ball to send it rattling past Davie Mathieson just eight minutes from time.

It could have been worse as Peterhead almost claimed victory two minutes later but Tommy Turner cleared a powerful Martin Johnston header off the line.

Mark Dobie put Gretna in front just before the break, stroking a penalty into the roof of the net after Mark Simpson had tripped John Hore.

Hore was inches from adding a second for Gretna in the 76th minute when he controlled the ball on his chest and fired in a 20-yard volley that left keeper Paul Mathers rooted to the spot but it shaved the bar.

Rowan then felt the players didn't show enough self-belief in the Scottish Cup as First Division Clyde came from behind at Raydale to secure a fourth-round tie against Motherwell.

"We got off to a great start but from that moment on we sat In front of our own 18-yard box and tried to soak up too much pressure," he said after the 2-1 defeat.

"The gap between the Divisions told in the end. We were chasing the ball for a lot of the game, but we didn't disgrace ourselves and had a few chances. Some of our players seemed a bit over-awed with the occasion."

Gretna went in front after just three minutes when Marc Cleeland played in Steve Skinner, who coolly finished from 10 yards.

Willie Falconer, Clyde's former Celtic striker, was the catalyst for the equaliser, his clever turn and powerful shot beaten out by David Mathieson for Andy Millen to slot in the rebound on the half hour.

Four minutes before the break Gretna midfielder Mick Galloway clipped a clever cross to the far post, Davie Irons headed into the danger area and top-scorer Mark Dobie's volley flew past the upright.

Clyde midfielder Paul Kane's deadball skills had been causing Gretna problems and in the 57th minute he curled over a free-kick from the right that was headed clear only as far as Millen, whose 20-yard snap-shot flew over the bar.

Two minutes later Kane sent over another free-kick and Alan Kernaghan's stooping header looped onto the roof of the net.

Just after the hour, Leigh Hinds got the winner with a sharp turn and low drive that flashed across Mathieson's dive and thumped in off the woodwork.

Dobie almost snatched a leveller with 15 minutes to go but his 25-yard drive went just wide.

Clyde player-boss Kernaghan admitted: "That's as poor as we've played all season, but we ground out a result in difficult conditions."

Gretna then picked up a point with a goalless home draw with Stirling, but Binos boss Allan Moore was amazed at referee Eddie Mack's controversial dismissal of debut boy Mark Crilly.

Crilly got his marching orders a minute before the break after clashing with David Irons. Moore said: "Mark knows he's let us down. The ref thought there was intent in his challenge. I'd just like to see consistency in decisions."

Stirling had two early chances through David O'Brien and Steve Kerrigan. Binos keeper Chris Reid had a lucky escape in the 57th minute when he spilled Mick Galloway's corner but the ball was scrambled off the line.

Rowan said after the stalemate: "We are lacking inventiveness."

Mark Dobie and Mick Galloway goals earned the club a point in a 2-2 draw at Elgin and Dobie and David Ormiston scored in a 2-1 win at East Stirling before another late, late goal denied Gretna in a 2-2 draw with Montrose. It was well into the 93rd minute when Graham McCheyne leapt highest to head in a Grant Johnson cross to grab a share of the points.

Gretna went in front in the third minute when Mick Galloway's bending free-kick flicked off the head of Graham Thomson and crashed into the roof of the net.

Brian Fairbairn doubled the advantage in the 21st minute when he robbed Thomson on the edge of the box and flashed in a low drive that keeper Gary McGlynn could not hold. Four minutes after the break Montrose pulled one back when McCheyne's long free-kick was flicked on and Gregor McKechnie poked in from close range.

Montrose almost levelled in the 69th minute but Dave Mathieson brilliantly tipped Kevin Webster's curling shot over. Gretna were reduced to ten men in the final minute when sub Steve Skinner was dismissed after clashing with Barry Donnachie.

John Hore hit the net in a 2-1 defeat at East Fife and was on target again in a 1-1 draw at Albion Rovers.

Dave McCallum then left Gretna's players and fans stunned as he netted an injury-time winner for Queen's Park. The Spiders full-back drilled in a 20-yard volley that clipped a defender and flashed low into the bottom corner of the net in the 93rd minute.

But Rowan Alexander breathed a sigh of relief as Gretna romped to their first home league win since August as they dumped East Stirling 3-1.

The manager was so disappointed with his side's home form that he named himself as a substitute. But he remained on the bench as two last-gasp strikes won it for the Borderers - and it could have been more. John Hore shot just wide and thumped a diving header inches over before he tucked away a Gavin Skelton cross for the opener in first half stoppage time.

'Shire keeper Chris Todd brilliantly turned a Ryan McGuffie volley wide and saw a deflected Davie Irons header rattle the woodwork before Gretna veteran striker Mark Dobie was sent off.

Stuart Kelly fired in a leveller from eight yards in the 75th minute. But McGuffie slotted Gretna back in front in the 89th minute from another whipped in Skelton centre. Then in the dying seconds youngster Wayne Gordon robbed a defender and ran half the length of the pitch before slipping in the third.

Eddie Annand then blasted home the only goal of a scrappy game to give promotion-chasing Morton a crucial 1-0 win at Raydale - and admitted he'd take six more wins like that if it meant going up.

Annand smashed Chris Miller's drilled cross into the top corner in the 55th minute to win it. Both sides hit the bar early on and Gretna's John Hore lofted a volley onto the roof of the net before his teenage strike partner Wayne Gordon missed a sitter. The youngster pounced on a short back pass to chip over keeper Craig Coyle but, with the goal gaping, he blasted an angled shot against the post. Gaffer Rowan Alexander wasn't too downbeat after the defeat and said: "The first half was the best we've played all season, we were lively, enthusiastic and moved the ball well."

But Gretna went down 1-0 at Peterhead when Andy Roddie's 52nd-minute corner was only half cleared and fell to Martin Johnston. His shot looked to be heading into the top corner, but Peterhead predator Iain Stewart flicked the ball in with his head to make sure.

And the late goal home hoodoo struck again in the next fixture as Ross Graham kept East Fife's title hopes on track with a last-gasp leveller from the penalty spot.

Graham struck after Kyle May had brought down sub Gordon Love in the 90th minute. Gretna had gone in front in the first minute when Keith Knox headed in a Mick Galloway corner and May made it 2-0 when keeper Jim Butter punched Galloway's free-kick onto his head.

James Herkes got East Fife back in it when he fired home Michael Hall's flick and Graham made it 2-2, heading in a Barry McLean cross. But Gavin Skelton forced in Gretna's third with just nine minutes left.

A 1-0 defeat followed at Stirling before Emilio Bottiglieri sent the Cappielow fans into raptures with a sensational strike as Morton took a step nearer Division Two with a convincing 5-0 win over Gretna.

Bottiglieri curled a right-foot drive from 22 yards into the top corner of the net in the 65th minute to finally finish the black and whites.

And that opened the floodgates as Morton went on to hammer in three more goals. Gretna had looked determined to upset Morton's promotion hopes but their hard-working defence was broken down after 33 minutes when Alex Williams drove in the opener through a crowded goalmouth.

Gretna threatened an equaliser after 55 minutes when Steve Skinner forced his way past three defenders but his shot was well saved by the diving Craig Coyle.

But it was the Bottiglieri strike which raised the temperature and just two minutes later Eddie Annand forced in a third for Morton from close range. John Maisano drove in the fourth after 75 minutes before Williams wrapped it up three minutes later.

In the final home game of the season Rowan Alexander grabbed Gretna's winner against Elgin after a Galloway penalty was touched onto the post. But sixty seconds later the ecstasy turned to agony as he was given a pain-killing injection after being stretchered off when he suffered a back spasm.

Gretna number two Derek Frye said: "Rowan has fire in his belly and we'll be looking for someone similar to lead the line next year."

Ryan McMullen fired Elgin in front in the 20th minute when Michael Sanderson sent him clear.

But Gretna levelled in the 40th minute when Steve Skinner fired into the bottom corner from 20 yards. Within a minute Skinner had jinked his way into the Elgin box only to be fouled by Fraser Bremner. Galloway's spot-kick was palmed onto the post and Alexander reacted quickest to smash in the rebound.

And Brian Fairbairn hit the only goal of the game as Gretna won at Montrose on the last day of the season. It was against the run of play when Fairbairn forced home a Steven Skinner cross from close range. The second half failed was drab and produced little in the way of goalmouth action, with Ralph Brand going closest for the home side from 30 yards. The club completed a decent first season in Scottish League football by finishing a respectable sixth, with Montrose one place behind them.

During the summer Brooks Mileson agreed to come on board full time at the club as Managing Director, and he wanted to do things the right way - pumping in a substantial amount of cash to turn the club full-time with Rowan Alexander unveiling a five-year plan to get the club into the Scottish Premier League.

Brooks would go on to build up a hugely successful community programme at Gretna with 112 schools attached providing free coaching, book clubs and drug education. Gretna would also fund a drug rehab centre in Dumfries, employ two schoolteachers on a part time basis to teach literacy, numeracy and I.T. skills.

Brooks was also very involved with football supporters' trusts in England and Scotland and is a huge supporter of non-league football both side of the border, helping out at over sixty clubs.

The extraordinary man was also involved in charity work covering support of the Rap Foundation in Romania, children's hospices and many animal welfare centres.

It was almost inevitable that when these two determined men got together that an amazing adventure was about to unfold.

Two

Season 2003/04

The Journey begins

DAVID HOLDSWORTH jokes that if he hadn't been a footballer, he'd have been a bank robber.

The strapping six-foot Londoner certainly looks the part and wouldn't be out of place on the set of a Guy Ritchie gangster movie.

It doesn't take a great deal of imagination to picture him as a likeable rogue alongside the likes of Vinnie Jones, Goldie or even Michael Caine in Get Carter or the Italian Job.

On his first match day at Raydale Park, the 35-year old central defender walked down past the small main stand in a stylish grey Crombie overcoat holding his boots between two fingers - but it could easily have been a double-barrelled sawn-off shotgun.

Holdsworth was born and brought up with his twin brother Dean on a tough council estate in Walthamstow in the capital, where the quickest way out is as a footballer, boxer or protection racketeer.

"I grew up in the West Ham area of East London which, like all cities, has it's good and bad parts," he said. "I supported West Ham from a young age and being a Hammer, I learned the culture of football."

It was through his love of the Claret and Blues that he took the football route and signed as an apprentice for Watford in 1986 with his brother. While Dean played just 20 games for the Hornets, David enjoyed a 10-year career at Vicarage Road, wracking up 303 appearances and scoring 13 goals.

He made a £450,000 move North to Sheffield United in 1996 and after 3 years and 113 games he was sold to Birmingham City for £1.25 million.

After playing more than 100 games for City, David had a brief loan spell at Walsall, played one game for Bolton Wanderers after a free transfer and then moved on to

Scarborough before Gretna's ambitious bid brought the Eastender to Gretna in the summer of 2003.

Holdsworth initially jetted up to Newcastle and drove across the Border to play for the Black and Whites before moving to the area.

"I'm thoroughly enjoying being here and we've overcome difficulties very quickly. You don't expect a team to gel straight away but we've put in some good performances and are hoping to build on that," said Holdsworth, who is sharp as a cut-throat razor, intelligent and funny.

"I don't think we can talk about winning the title just yet. The players are having to adapt to a pro basis as it's the first time some of them have played full-time, but around Christmas we should see the bigger picture for this season."

Holdsworth exerts a cool confidence on the pitch in a black and white shirt offering words of encouragement, telling his team-mates to keep it tight, gesturing with his hands and timing tackles to perfection. He's never flustered and is a model experienced pro.

Off the field, Holdsworth looks smart in his grey club suit and blue shirt with the glint of a chunky silver watch past his cuff, his short, black hair neatly combed in a side parting. He enjoys Italian food and black coffee and his favourite actors are Hollywood hardmen Robert De Niro and Al Pacino.

"I thought De Niro was absolutely fantastic in Goodfellas and the Godfather is one of my favourite films. All of them gangster movies typify team spirit and you get on a lot further if you try and do things like that - by sticking together."

Instead of cracking safes and robbing bundles of bank notes, Holdsworth loves nothing better than stealing the ball off a centre forward. And if he mis-times a tackle and fouls, maybe boss Rowan Alexander could be heard muttering: "You're only supposed to take the bloody ball off him!" in a Michael Caine-style from the dug-out.

Manager Alexander made a number of other big-name signings as the Raydale revolution began apace with supremo Brooks Mileson coming on-board as Managing Director during the summer and changing the club to a limited company. "The past has been forgotten and credit to all the volunteers who took the club as far as they could. The good times are about to unfold before our very eyes, and very quickly, we anticipate," said Alexander.

David's striker brother Dean was almost captured, but big centre forward Martin Cameron was signed from St. Mirren and experienced former Hibs, Partick Thistle and Raith Rovers midfielder Danny Lennon came on board. Lee Maddison was also signed from neighbours Carlisle United and quick and skilful young striker Gary Cohen was snapped up from Scarborough. James Allen joined from Queen's Park, and Paul O'Neill, Richard Prokas and Ricky Robb were all signed.

Brooks and the managements determination to do things right saw the players going full-time but the campaign got off to a disappointing start as First Division Caley Thistle's quality proved too hot for Gretna to handle as they eased into the Second Round of the Bell's Cup with a 5-0 win at Raydale.

Gretna had survived a penalty appeal when Rob McBain went down under a challenge from on-loan St. Mirren defender Ricky Robb before ex-Livingston star David Bingham chipped in the opener from 20 yards in the 23rd minute.

The black and whites almost levelled four minutes before the break when James Allan and Martin Cameron combined to feed Gavin Skelton, but his low drive flashed inches wide.

Steven Hislop thumped a shot against the Gretna woodwork just after the break - but he only had to wait five minutes to celebrate adding the second.

Keeper Davie Mathieson uncharacteristically blundered, kicking fresh air and leaving Hislop the simple task of tapping into the empty net.

Paul Ritchie leapt to powerfully head in a McBain corner for the third in the 56th minute and Richard Hart squeezed the fourth under Mathieson six minutes later.

Hart piled on the agony and completed the rout in the 82nd minute when he swept in a Bingham cross from 12 yards.

Midfielder James Allen didn't have long to wait to play his old club as the Spiders were at Raydale Park for the League opener - and he was left gutted as they snatched a point with a stunning last gasp strike.

Allen had been desperate to put one over his former buddies and admitted he had had dreams about scoring the winner.

But he watched in horror from the dug-out after being subbed as Spiders sub Frankie Carroll grabbed a share of the points with a superb volley.

"It was quite funny to be playing my old club on the first day of the season, but I had been looking forward to it," said Allen.

"There are lots of the same boys from last year at the club so I was keen to do well and dreamed of scoring the winner - but it just wasn't to be."

Gaffer Rowan Alexander was stunned as his new look side once again fell to the late goal syndrome that plagued his side the previous season.

"You expect experienced players like we've got to be able to kill time, but we gave them too much time," he said.

"It was an untidy game and there wasn't any fluency. The one or two times we did play with some fluency we created chances and Martin Cameron could have won it."

Cameron fired in what Gretna thought would prove to be the winner in the 81st minute. Strike partner Gary Cohen robbed Dinning and whipped over a centre that Cameron put into the net from close range.

But four minutes into stoppage time, with the Gretna management screaming at the players to concentrate, Carroll latched onto a long ball and blasted a stunning volley into the corner of the net past Davie Mathieson.

Peterhead took the points with a 2-0 win at Balmoor in the next game before Ryan Baldacchino and Mark Birch were added to the side from neighbours Carlisle United. And Birch proved lightning can strike twice as he fired an unstoppable dream debut goal in a 1-1 draw at home to Dumfries & Galloway derby rivals Stranraer.

The former Carlisle full-back had scored just once in three years at Brunton Park but showed his sensational effort was more than just a flash in the pan as he forced keeper Andy McCondichie into three great saves with more fierce long range efforts.

Birch blasted Gretna in front in the 68th minute with a 20-yard drive and raced to the dug-out, where he leapt up and punched the air in celebration before being mobbed by his team-mates.

"It sat up well and I just closed my eyes and hit it," he admitted.

"I don't get many goals so I don't remember the celebration - the last time I think I just put my hand up and walked away. Hopefully I can get a few more for the club."

Ten minutes after his wonder strike, Birch unleashed 35-yard thunderbolt that had McCondichie sprawling to save and with three minutes remaining he smashed a 22-yard free kick that the keeper did well to parry.

Gretna boss Rowan Alexander was delighted with the contributions of both Birch and fellow new boy Ryan Baldacchino, whose pace, skill and crossing proved a thorn in the side of the Stranraer defence all afternoon.

But he was bitterly disappointed with a Gary Cohen miss that could have won the game.

Just four minutes after Birch had struck, Cohen latched onto a through ball and raced through on goal but McCondichie read him as he attempted to slip the ball past him and saved with an outstretched foot.

"We let them off the hook," said Alexander.

"Cohen missed a sitter. He tried to be clever when he should have just rolled it into the net. It infuriates me that we didn't kill them off. The players have to shape up and do the business or they're out - simple as that."

"We did produce some exciting play down the flanks and I was really, really pleased with Birch and Baldacchino. They shouldn't really be playing at this level. Martin Cameron was exceptional as well and I wish I was ten years younger, as I would love to play alongside a player like that."

Cameron could have shot Gretna ahead in the 10th minute but blasted Baldacchino's low centre over the bar from 12 yards.

Former Hamilton hit-man Michael Moore proved a handful at the other end and he ensured that David Holdsworth had to be at his best.

In the 36th minute Birch drilled in a low 25-yarder that the diving McCondichie parried before it was cleared.

Just before the break John Hore played in Ryan McGuffie, who span and teed up Cameron but his shot lacked power and was saved comfortably by the goalkeeper.

Stranraer midfielder Allan Jenkins had his head in his hands in the 52nd minute when Allan Grant headed on to him and his sweet half volley flashed inches over.

But Grant was smiling just two minutes after Cohen's miss when he broke free down the left and shot low across Dave Mathieson to level.

Gavin Skelton almost won it for Gretna but his shot was turned away one handed by McCondichie.

The first win came at Raydale Park with a 3-1 success that saw hit-man Martin Cameron claim the match ball after smashing in a hat-trick to demolish an Albion Rovers side that by full-time had been reduced to nine men and had a coach dismissed from the dugout.

His delighted skipper Mick Galloway said afterwards: "When Martin came to the club there was a lot of pressure on his shoulders with his goalscoring record and people were expecting a lot from him. When he got his first two goals you could see the hunger in his eyes to get the third."

The 25-year-old former St. Mirren goal-ace hit 19 goals in 30 appearances at Love Street the previous season and had netted 50 times in two seasons with Alloa Athletic.

He almost fired Gretna into an early lead when he latched onto Jedd Stirling's loose pass but keeper Chris Fahey got down quickly to parry away his powerful shot.

Soon after Ryan Baldacchino beat two men inside the area but dragged his angled shot and the grateful Fahey's arms and then Cameron's live-wire strike partner Gary Cohen had the crowd on their feet with a 20-yard drive that flashed just wide.

In the 32nd minute Mark Birch threaded an inch perfect through ball for Cohen whose attempt to nick the ball past the outrushing Fahey clipped the keeper's leg and Cameron coolly fired the rebound into the empty net from 20 yards.

If the big, shaven-headed hot-shot was happy with that strike, his smile was even bigger just three minutes later as Mark

Eccles did well to get into the box with a solo run and shot that Fahey dived to parry and Cameron was on the spot to blast number two into the roof of the net.

Fahey then made a fantastic triple save to deny Cohen, Cameron and Galloway as shots pinballed around the box in a goalmouth scramble.

Such was Gretna's dominance that keeper Dave Mathieson smiled and waved as a David Farrell 30-yard free kick sailed well over the bar.

And Cameron allowed himself a little grin at the other end when, on the stroke of half time, as the ball fell invitingly on the volley, he spotted Fahey off his line and went for glory but sliced horribly wide.

Seconds after the break Rovers bulky striker Mark Yardley clashed with Galloway on the edge of the Gretna box and was sent off.

Surprisingly, this inspired the Cliftonhill side's best spell with sub Kevin McAllister - the former Hibs, Chelsea and Falkirk man - driving them on. In the 50th minute Paul McManus crossed from the right and Iain Diack blasted in a shot that rattled back off the underside of the bar, stuck the diving Mathieson and rolled into the corner of the net.

But Gretna had banished the defensive gremlins and inability to kill teams off that had plagued them and Dave Irons sent a beautiful 40 yard pass to the feet of Eccles who touched back to Cameron to curl in an inviting cross that just eluded the inrushing Cohen.

"There was a bit of slackness and a loss of concentration that let them back in it - they might have felt it was easier playing against ten men," said gaffer Rowan Alexander.

"But there was enough experience and quality out there to make sure panic didn't set in as it sometimes has in the past."

"That was our best display of the season. We destroyed them down the flanks where Baldacchino and Eccles were tremendous and Martin Cameron took his goals well."

Mark Birch tried his luck from 25-yards with a thunderbolt that zipped inches past the post, and any

Rovers hopes of a comeback were dashed in the 73rd as

Sterling, who'd been run ragged by Baldacchino, fouled the former Carlisle player and was given his marching orders.

Two minutes later Andy Paterson tripped Cohen in the box and Cameron stepped up to drill home the spot-kick and seal the win.

But Gretna went out of the CIS Cup at the first hurdle as they suffered last-minute goal heartache once again as Peterhead's Ian Stewart rifled a shot in off the woodwork with the last kick of the game to send the Borderers crashing out.

The former Inverness Caledonian Thistle ace struck twice in the final eight minutes and admitted that the last thing the Blue Toon wanted was extra time with a lengthy coach trip back to Aberdeenshire awaiting them on a Tuesday night.

"It's great to win any game in the last minute," said goal hero Stewart, who took his tally to 51 in three years for the club.

"I missed a couple of chances during the game, but then I've missed enough over the years to know that you just keep going and hope that you put one away - even Henrik Larsson misses chances. I took a bad touch and took four players with me, the shot hit the inside of the post and it was brilliant to see it roll into the net. We're looking to get a Premier League team in the next round to get a bit of money for the club."

Gretna began brightly with cultured midfielder Mick Galloway, wearing the captains armband, spraying passes around the park with both the outside of his boot and his instep with a pinpoint accuracy that dictated the play.

Veteran David Irons took a leaf from his skipper's book with a long ball to release Ryan Baldacchino who touched inside to Martin Cameron. The big hitman turned defender Shaun McSkimming but blasted over from the edge of the box.

Cameron, who did a four-year apprenticeship as a butcher and would not be hard to imagine in a blood-splattered apron, showed there is a lot more to his game than just goalscoring as on several occasions he showed excellent control and awareness to release wing pair Baldacchino and Mark Eccles.

Eccles beat four men down the left in the 19th minute but his shot from 18 yards under pressure was disappointing and went straight at keeper Paul Mathers.

At the other end Robbie Raeside split the Gretna defence with a great ball but Irons blocked Martin Bavidge's shot. The ball broke to Daryl Smith who crossed and keeper Davie Mathieson saved brilliantly one-handed from the stretching Bavidge from three yards out.

Gretna went one up just a minute later when Baldacchino crossed and Ryan McGuffie ghosted unmarked into the Peterhead box to side-foot a composed 12-yard volley into the bottom corner of the net giving Mathers no chance.

The former Newcastle player almost made it a double in the 26th minute when Gary Cohen ran into trouble and as the ball broke free McGuffie smashed in a shot that clipped off a defender and flew agonisingly wide.

Mathieson was again called into action, turning a Bavidge shot into the side netting as the striker got in behind the solid-looking Gretna defence for just the second time.

Galloway then sent a perfect pass to Baldacchino who was forced all the way across the Peterhead box and laid-off for Eccles to curl in a centre that Cameron rose to meet with a thumping header that shaved the bar.

Just on half time, Lee Maddison raced half the length of the pitch and played to Cameron who's neat touch and clever turn released Baldacchino to unleash a curling drive that Mathers smothered.

But after the break Smith drilled straight into Mathieson's midrift and then Stewart hit a dipping volley over the bar with the goal at his mercy as Peterhead signalled their intent.

Cohen's strong running was almost rewarded with a goal in the 54th minute, but his curling 20 yard shot went just over the angle of bar and post and ten minutes later he stretched but just couldn't reach an Eccles cross that flashed across the face of goal.

Raeside should have equalised when he rose unmarked from a corner but powered his header well wide and in the 76th minute, with Gretna hanging on, he again headed goalwards and the experienced, cool-headed David Holdsworth hooked clear in the danger area.

There was a sense of inevitability as Stewart levelled in the 82nd minute when the ball broke free on the left edge of the box and he swivelled and drilled a low shot across Mathieson into the corner of the net.

But Irons almost won it for Gretna just a minute later as he ran from the half-way line and, as the defenders backed off, he fired a 25 yard shot that beat the diving Mathers but flew inches wide and smacked back off the advertising hoardings.

In the final minute Cameron touched back to sub Gavin Skelton to whip in a dangerous, looping cross that just evaded McGuffie who was straining every muscle in his neck to try and get on the end of it.

With the last kick of the game Stewart, surrounded by defenders, fired in a 20 yard shot that smashed off the inside of the post, hit Mathieson and bobbled into the net to silence Raydale with a sickening sense of Deja-Vu.

Defender Mark Birch said: "We're gutted. When we were 1-0 up we gave the ball away a bit too much and we should have kept it a lot more. It was end-to-end football, but we've got to be a bit tighter and shut up shop a little bit. It's too cavalier."

"The first half we played well but we set our standards on Saturday and we let ourselves down a bit from those standards that we set."

"The league's the most important thing but I think it's good for the club if we could have had a bit of a cup run. But it's not to be so we've just got to concentrate on the league."

Cameron hit two more and Ryan McGuffie was also on target in a 3-3 draw at Elgin before McGuffie hit the winner in a 1-0 success at Cowdenbeath.

Leaders Stirling then visited Raydale and Top gun Martin Cameron was then just inches from salvaging a point for Gretna but a Colin McKinnon strike condemned the Borderers to their first home defeat of the season and sent Bino's five points clear at the top of the table.

In the dying seconds, sub Gary Cohen made a strong run down the right and touched back to Mick Galloway who bent in a cross that Cameron rose to meet ten yards from goal.

His powerful header left keeper Myles Hogarth stranded, but looped agonisingly just over the bar and onto the roof of the net.

And just before the final whistle sub Ian Stevens worked himself a bit of space and let fly from the edge of the box, but Hogarth got down smartly to smother and Gretna's last chance was gone.

Stirling began brightly with some crisp passing moves and former Hearts player Ryan Davidson created their first real chance in the 11th minute when his dangerous cross was half cleared by Mark Birch and goal-hero McKinnon fired in an 18-yarder that Dave Mathieson saved well diving to his left.

Bino's hit-men Davidson and Scott McLean were looking dangerous but were well marshalled by veterans Dave Irons and David Holdsworth all afternoon.

In the 23rd minute McLean cleverly span Holdsworth and released David O'Brien but his low cross was hooked clear by Irons as the defensive pair provided a strong unit throughout the end-to-end encounter.

Wing-ace Ryan Baldacchino menaced the Stirling defence with his pace at the other end and after robbing Derek Anderson, as four Bino's defenders went to him, he squared to Ryan McGuffie who's attempted chip went straight at Hogarth.

McLean thought he'd broken the deadlock on the half hour when he fired an unstoppable, bending shot into the top corner from 20 yards, but the linesman had his flag raised for offside during the build up.

The same linesman, although he was brave in holding his flag up for so long on that occasion, would later infuriate Gretna boss Rowan Alexander with a string of contentious decisions.

Three minutes later former Celtic defender Mark McNally, who was a rock at the heart of the visitors defence, sliced a clearance and Hogarth had to dive and fingertip away at full stretch with Wayne Gordon set to pounce.

Gretna finished the half strongly and on-loan Carlisle ace Baldacchino twice went close, drilling a low shot through a crowd of players that Hogarth saw late but got down to save.

Then McGuffie sent him clear with a defence splitting through ball but his angled drive was beaten away by the keeper.

In the 50th minute sharp-thinking Cameron started a move with a quick free kick and as Lee Maddison swung over a cross he leapt to get on the end of it, but his header fell just wide.

In the 64th minute Paul Nugent almost sent McKinnon clear but Holdsworth was across quickly to clear the danger and a couple of minutes later the former Watford man again showed his class as he sent a fantastic 40-yard diagonal ball to the feet of Baldacchino.

But that was one of the rare occasions in the second half that the flying winger, who had posed such a threat in the opening period, would receive the ball as Stirling snuffed out the danger.

The league leaders grabbed the winner in the 79th minute when Andrew Gibson flighted over a right wing cross and Davidson's knock down was deflected into the path of McKinnon who rammed into the roof of the net from close range to spark the celebrations.

Gretna's frustration was clear and five minutes later sub Richard Prokas had his name scribbled in the referees notebook for a foul that left Andrew Smith rolling on the turf in agony.

Rowan Alexander said that Gretna looked like a Championship-winning side for eleven minutes - but admitted that after that they were very poor as Montrose lifted themselves off the ropes to snatch a point in a 1-1 draw at Raydale.

Martin Cameron had headed the Borderers in front as they dominated but a lucky deflection got the Gable Endies back in it.

"For the first eleven minutes we were different class and we had four or five chances to win the game during that time," said the Gretna gaffer.

"But then they got very blasé and I'm annoyed at the players for letting the game slip from their grasp. I'm the one getting the stick from the supporters and that annoys me. I wish I was 20 years younger and on the pitch so I could knock some of our lads heads together."

Gretna were simply phenomenal from the kick off and it looked a simple case of how many as Montrose struggled to cope with the Borderers pace, vision and movement.

In the second minute full back Mark Birch got in behind the Montrose defence and fired in a low centre that keeper Jim Butter parried and a defender deflected Mick Galloway's follow up into the path of Gavin Skelton whose drive was blocked.

Moments later Cameron shaved the bar with a powerful drive then Ryan Baldacchino had a low shot deflected wide.

Galloway bent in the resultant corner and David Holdsworth's powerful header was cleared off the line by a Montrose trialist.

Skelton, in for Mark Eccles, looked keen to hang onto the number 11 shirt after being handed his chance and went past the visiting full back with a quick turn and burst of speed but his low drive flashed agonisingly across the face of goal after beating Butter at his near post.

The opener finally came in the 11th minute when Galloway curled in a free kick and Cameron's thumping downward header looped into the corner of the net for his seventh goal of the season.

Cameron then had a header cleared off the line by John McQuillan and headed a Skelton cross onto the roof of the net as Gretna kept up the pressure.

In the 24th minute Wayne Gordon robbed Craig Farnan in the Gretna half and embarked on a solo run at pace, going past Mark Simpson like he wasn't there, but his finish was disappointing and dragged wide from the edge of the box.

Holdworth then launched himself at a Skelton corner but his header went just wide.

Montrose should have levelled 12 minutes later as Gretna inexplicably took their foot of the gas - but the finish was straight out of Carry On Football.

The ball broke free in the box but Steve Kerrigan and Kevin Webster collided with the goal gaping and it trickled harmlessly wide.

Webster made amends right on half time when he fired in a curling 25 yarder that keeper Dave Mathieson brilliantly tipped over one-handed at full stretch.

From the resulting corner Mathieson got a hand to Simpson's close range header but the ball came back off the post and rebounded into the net off the unlucky Dave Irons.

The second half was a much more even affair and Gretna had Richard Prokas to thank in the 70th minute when he hooked a Keith Gibson shot off the line.

Two minutes later Baldachinno whipped in a free kick and Holdsworth's towering header smacked off the woodwork and left the bar reverberating like a tuning fork.

It was tough luck on the former Watford, Sheffield United and Birmingham ace who produced another man-of-the-match performance and looked like a Championship winner all game.

With five minutes to go Irons flicked on Lee Maddison's corner and as Holdsworth went up with Butter the keeper punched clear.

Galloway went to place his shot into the bottom corner from 20 yards but Butter scrambled across goal and parried away at the foot of the post.

And Gretna were made to battle all the way for a 1-0 victory against a plucky East Stirling side who belied their bottom of the league placing. Gretna's cause was not helped by having to play the final twenty-five minutes with only ten men following Gary Cohen's red card for a retaliatory kick at 'Shires Graham McGhee.

The opening exchanges were even with both sides scorning good scoring chances. On the half-hour David Mathieson produced the save of the match to push away a Jamie McKay free-kick which had taken a wicked deflection. It was hardly surprising with the laxity in front of goal that the first half ended goal-less.

Martin Cameron should have broken the deadlock immediately after the break when he pounced on a slack clearance but he delayed his shot and the danger was cleared. 'Shire broke upfield and Scott Livingston's low cross caused panic in the Gretna defence before Mathieson pounced on the ball.

The only goal came on 55 minutes when Ryan Baldacchino headed Lee Maddison's cross down to Ian Stevens who applied a wicked back-spin to the ball which deceived Connolly in the 'Shire goal.

Gary Cohen had been on the field a mere 13 minutes and it proved unlucky for him when he aimed a kick in retaliation after appearing to be fouled by Graham McGhee. The loss of a player seemed to galvanise Gretna and Baldacchino was unlucky to see his swerving shot hit the bar with ten minutes left but the single goal was to prove enough.

Lee Maddison was no stranger to Scottish football when he joined the club back in the August.

The classy full-back spent four years at Dens Park playing in the top-flight with Dundee and admits it was a fantastic experience turning out against some of the biggest names in the game.

But Maddison, who cultured left boot was capable of arrowing 40-yard defence-splitting balls across the pitch, was happy to be pulling on the Black and White shirt at Raydale.

"I'm enjoying it at Gretna. It's a lot different to being at Carlisle; it's more relaxed here and it's a much more friendly place to be. It's great," he said.

"The Scottish Third Division is a little bit quicker than the Third Division down in England and that took a bit of addressing and getting used to. There's no-one that we should really be wary of out of the teams we've played so far and hopefully, when we get used to the team that's being built at the moment, we'll be in full flow."

"I spent four years at Dundee and three of those were in the Premier League so it was great playing against the likes of Larsson, Kanchelskis and people like that. I was disappointed to leave at the end. The new manager came in, an Italian guy who tended to bring in a lot of foreign players, and sort of pushed all the British lads out. But you have to move on from those sort of things, so it was just a matter of going down to Carlisle and getting on with my career again," continued Maddison.

Dundee's then Capo Ivano Bonetti would eventually sign Beto Carranza and Argentinian World Cup ace Claudio Caniggia for the Dark Blues as the British players moved on.

Maddison was keen to pick up some silverware for the Borderers and said: "Our ambition for this season is promotion. Definitely. There's no-one in this league we should be frightened of. Whether it's top or second place, as long as we're promoted, I think that's the most important thing for the club this year."

Gretna secured three important points with a 3-2 win at home to Peterhead when striker Martin Cameron stooped to glance in the winner with just sixty seconds remaining - and admitted that he didn't realise the ball was in the net until he heard everyone screaming.

"We knew it was going to be a hard game and we're absolutely delighted to get the three points," said Cameron, whose two-goal haul took his tally to nine in ten games.

"Hopefully the result will get us going. The spirit at the club is good and hopefully we can continue it," he added.

Gretna gaffer Rowan Alexander was equally delighted and said: "We've been working in training with Martin to get to the near post and he's done it, got in front of his man and won it for us."

Lee Maddison curled in a teasing centre from the left and Cameron's glancing header beat keeper Paul Mathers to send Raydale Park into raptures.

It was a stark contrast to the near silence that greeted Iain Stewart's opener in the 19th minute.

Keiran McGuiness sliced on Andy Roddie's corner and the former Inverness Caley Thistle striker headed in off the underside of the bar from close range.

Martin Bavidge then almost made it 2-0 when he raced clear but his low drive was brilliantly turned around the post by keeper Dave Mathieson.

Gretna came into it more in the lead up to the break as Mathers was forced to turn a Cameron header over the bar then Gavin Skelton headed a Ryan Baldacchino cross back to Ian Stevens, whose close range header was deflected over.

"It was a game of two halves," said boss Alexander

"In the first we weren't at the races and they came out of the traps and destroyed us. We were lucky to be just 1-0 down at half time. We gave the lads a right good talking too during the break and told them to work harder, close men down and push the game from the front - and that's what got them the result. We showed great character to come back into it."

Cameron took just 21 seconds to level after the interval as Stevens' shot was deflected into his path and he fired into the corner of the net from four yards.

Three minutes later Richard Prokas was desperately unlucky not to get on the scoresheet as he shaved the bar with a fierce volley from 20 yards.

The tireless midfield battler was getting into forward positions with increasing frequency as Gretna camped in the Peterhead half and he almost got on the end of a Cameron knock-on, but Mathers was out quickly to clear.

In the 74th minute a Baldacchino cross caused confusion in the Blue Toon box and Skelton battled to stab home from six yards.

While it looked like the winger had won it, nine minutes later Gretna failed to clear a corner and Graeme Stewart smacked a low volley through a crowd of players and into the corner of the net to level.

But the Borderers refused to crumble and Cameron, who was sporting a gash above his right eye from last weeks victory at East Stirling, was mobbed by his team-mates after pouncing at the death.

And Gretna's third win in succession was even more emphatic than the 1-0 scoreline suggested at Queen's Park and ensured their promotion push stayed firmly on track. The Raydale men totally dominated proceedings from start to finish and but for a combination of good goalkeeping and a couple of debatable offside decisions the margin of victory would have been much greater.

Ian Stevens and Richard Prokas came close in the opening minutes and Queens keeper Scrimgeour saved a David Irons effort at the second attempt. The home keeper again did well on the half hour to foil Stevens. Gretna looked to have gone ahead after 34 minutes when Martin Cameron headed home Gavin Skelton's cross but the assistant's flag quickly shot up to deny the big striker. Queens only chance of the first half came two minutes later when McAuley broke clear only to see David Mathieson come to Gretna's rescue.

Gretna got in the groove right from the restart and Cameron flicked on a Baldacchino cross to Mick Galloway who headed in from close range but again the assistant's flag came to the home side's rescue. Prokas had a shot saved on the hour and Baldacchino saw a fierce drive tipped over by Scrimgeour.

The breakthrough came with ten minutes remaining when Galloway's left wing corner was headed in by goal-machine

Cameron. Queens had little to offer in reply and Ally Graham's late effort failed to trouble Mathieson.

Gretna were also given a boost as Danny Lennon and John Hore continued to work their way back to fitness following their long-term injury hell.

Lennon had been out of action for two months with an ankle problem and had spent a week at the FA Sports Injury centre at Lilleshall, while Hore had a successful operation on a troublesome knee.

"It was a change at Lilleshall for me and a good change of atmosphere," said influential former Partick skipper Lennon.

"Everybody that was down their was in the same position with long-term injuries. They looked at me and where I was unstable at certain things they put me on a programme, which has been going great. I had the full weekend off which I think has done me the world of good as well. Although it's been a very hard week, I think it's served its purpose and hopefully I can kick on again this week," he continued.

"The lowest point is not Saturday's because when the lads are winning I'm delighted for them. I think the low point for me is Gretna have given me a good deal down here and I haven't produced anything for them yet. To see them struggle early doors and not get off to the start we would have liked, although we're climbing there now, that's been the most frustrating bit - seeing that happen and knowing that I couldn't do anything about it."

"it's been very frustrating, but , to be fair to the lads and the gaffer, over the last two or three weeks everybody's raring to go and are showing determination and long may it continue," said the experienced midfielder.

"I'm absolutely champing at the bit to get back into action and now that I have come this far I'd just like to take my time and make sure it's bang on rather than just diving straight in. I've been speaking to the medical team and they're happy with the way it's going and they've put me on an anti-inflammatory course because I was still felling pain when I was striking the ball, but it looks as though they've kicked in a bit. I'm pleasantly surprised how it has settled down."

Striker John Hore had been missing since August and had keyhole surgery on his knee.

"The operation's been a big success and I've come back a lot quicker after it," he said.

"The doctors have said that everything's gone well and that my knee looks in a good state, so I'm just looking at getting back as fast as I can. It's been the worst really, watching the lads from the stand - I've struggled badly," admitted the 21-year-old former Carlisle United man.

"Recently has been OK because I've known how long until I get back, but before the operation, when I didn't know what was wrong, I was a bit worried and I didn't know what was going on so that's when I was really struggling. But since I started running again and getting out in the fresh air, I've felt a lot better."

Hore was eagerly-anticipating the chance to play alongside top-gun Martin Cameron when he had fully recovered, and joked: "He's banging in all the goals, so hopefully I can take a few off him and share them around the team a bit!"

"Martin's a good player, everything's going to drop off him and he causes a lot of hassle so hopefully I'll get a few goals off him - and also create a few more chances for him."

An unstoppable Allistair McMillan rocket free-kick grabbed a share of the points for Elgin City in a 2-2 draw at Raydale.

The big defender stepped up to hammer the ball into the top corner of the net from fully 35 yards in the 71st minute, sparking mad celebrations from the visitors.

Elgin had survived an early scare when Craig Campbell headed Martin Cameron's powerful header from a Gavin Skelton corner off the line at the back post.

And they took a shock lead in the 25th minute when skipper Mick Galloway slipped in the middle of the park and his mis-placed pass was knocked in to lanky striker Chris Ogboke.

The youngster fired in an 18-yard shot that clipped off a defender and looped over keeper Dave Mathieson and high into the net.

Gretna levelled seven minutes later when Cameron's flick on sent Ian Stevens clear and, as he shaped to shoot, Jamie White brought him down with a clumsy challenge.

Cameron stepped up and sent Andy Goram the wrong way from the penalty spot to fire in his 11th goal of the season.

Four minutes before the break Gretna went in front when Gavin Skelton's deep cross from the left evaded White and Cameron controlled on his knee and coolly drilled low into the corner.

Gretna continued to look menacing after half time with winger Ryan Baldacchino tormenting the City defence.

In the 52nd minute he beat two men and whipped in a dangerous centre that McMillan cleared over his own bar with a diving header.

Galloway curled in the resulting corner and David Holdsworth rose unchallenged at the far post but headed wide from a great position.

The Borderers went close again in the 56th minute when Baldacchino crossed and Stevens' first time shot from 18 yards hit the bar.

Gretna took their foot off the gas after that and Elgin sub Alex Bone should have equalised when he raced through on goal but Mathieson stood his ground and saved well low to his left.

But Mathieson stood no chance with McMillan's exocet leveller that whistled past his despairing dive and thumped into the roof of the net.

City keeper Andy Goram, the former Rangers, Manchester United and Scotland star, said afterwards: "When we go forward we're not bad and if we can cut out the mistakes at the back we'll be alright. We've had a bit of luck to turn it around today and it's a good result for us as Gretna are a good side. I love playing football - that's it. If I was sat at home watching teletext today I'd be sick as a parrot as I know I can still play."

The 39-year-old took time to sign autographs and pose for photographs with fans after the game, as well as stopping to give interviews to the local press pack.

Goram, in an open-necked white shirt with his hair swept back, joked and chatted with fans and journalists beside the black metal rails of the dressing room tunnel for around fifteen minutes, and tipped Gretna to be in the running for promotion at the end of the season.

"Gretna have every chance of going up," he said. "They have a great striker, a tricky winger and plenty of experience at the back. Martin Cameron is a huge asset to them and their goalkeeper Davie Mathieson looks lively and doesn't make mistakes. From what I have seen out there, I would say they will be there or thereabouts at the end of the season."

Gretna then made light of the horrendous conditions at rain-drenched Cliftonhill to record a comprehensive 3-1 victory over Albion Rovers and keep their promotion charge on course.

In the opening ten minutes Gavin Skelton came close and Ryan Baldacchino had a cross-cum-shot tipped over by Bennett in the Rovers goal. The home side then enjoyed a spell of pressure with David Mathieson producing the save of the game when he punched over a Jordan Smith header at point-blank range.

Gretna regained their composure and took the lead after 27minutes when man-of-the-match Baldacchino crossed from the right for Ian Stevens to head past the static Bennett. From the restart a Rovers corner was only cleared as far as veteran Kevin McAllister who saw Mathieson block his shot with his foot.

The game was effectively over two minutes into the second half when Gavin Skelton's low drive from just outside the box skidded past Bennett. The Raydale men were in total command and David Irons had an effort cleared off the line before Ian Stevens fired over from a good position.

Stevens, however, made no mistake after 66 minutes when he turned to hammer home from 12 yards.

Rovers were reduced to 10 men on 78 minutes when John McCaig received his second yellow card as Gretna's flowing football continued to frustrate the home side. Rovers grabbed a consolation goal with three minutes left when Irons was harshly adjudged to have fouled McAllister and Jered Stirling stepped up to deprive Mathieson of his clean sheet.

Gretna sent out a warning to the rest of the Third Division as they demolished Second Division Dumbarton and sent the Sons crashing out of the Tennent's Scottish Cup 4-0 at Raydale.

It was only a matter of time before the signings made by Rowan Alexander gelled - and the Gretna gaffer, with new

Technical Director David Wilkes alongside him in the dug-out, got their homework spot-on to send Raydale into raptures.

The Borderers grabbed an early lead in the sixth minute as Mick Galloway played in Ian Stevens and the veteran striker didn't break stride as he drilled a low shot past keeper Stephen Grindlay from the edge of the box.

It was almost two six minutes later when Ryan Baldacchino's free-kick was cleared only as far as Richard Prokas, whose low volley was turned around the post by the sprawling keeper. Prokas hooked the resulting corner just over the bar from 12 yards as he ghosted unmarked into the box.

Dumbarton striker Emeka Obidile produced some good work in the middle of the park to release John Dillon in the 23rd minute, but his angled drive flashed harmlessly across the face of goal.

Five minutes later Martin Cameron flicked on a long ball and as Gavin Skelton and Criag McEwan challenged, outrushing keeper Findlay was caught by a boot and gashed above the eye, having to be replaced by former Rangers youngster Richard White between the posts.

White's first touch saw him perform acrobatics to brilliantly palm away a clever Cameron flicked header at full stretch. And five minutes before the break White again did well to produce a diving save from a side-footed Cameron far post volley.

Cameron did beat the youngster right on half time when he rose to meet Lee Maddison's whipped in centre, but his looping header smacked back off the crossbar.

Dumbarton came into the game more in the second half and could have levelled in the 66th minute, but sub Iain Russell headed Steven Bonar's cross wide from a great position. And sixty seconds later Obidile produced a burst of speed to race clear into the Gretna box but David Holdsworth made a fantastic last-ditch tackle to deny him a shooting opportunity.

And then a bolt from the blue stunned the visitors. There seemed little danger as sub James Allan played in to Gavin Skelton 35 yards from goal, but the midfielder let fly with a rocket shot that flashed past a stunned White and into the corner of the net.

The former electrician had been creating sparks on the pitch since his return to full-time football and Gary Cohen said of Skelton's wonder-strike: "I was warming up alongside where Gavin struck the ball from. It's come across him, he's hit it, and I looked at the keeper and thought 'ah, it's going wide,' but it's nestled neatly in the bottom corner."

"The first thing I did was run and jump up and celebrate - I wanted to run on the pitch, but you can't do that! He does it quite often in training, so you never know if he'll score a better one. If you've done it once, you can do it again."

In the 80th minute David Holdsworth leapt to flick a header past White that was cleared off the line and hacked clear for another corner. This time Holdsworth made no mistake and powered a thumping header home from 8 yards.

Gretna piled on the agony for Dumbarton and added a fourth with four minutes remaining as Allan embarked on a great solo run down the right before teeing up fellow sub Wayne Gordon who showed coolness and composure to chip into the net.

Brian Wake then signed for the club from Carlisle, linking up with former Tow Law Town team-mate Mark Eccles after signing a three-and-a-half year deal.

His former Carlisle team-mate Ryan Baldacchino fired in an early winner as title-chasing Gretna dug deep for the three points that moved them back into third spot with a 1-0 win over Cowdenbeath.

The Borderers had been denied a dream start as hit man Martin Cameron's clever back heel from a Baldacchino cross beat keeper Andrew Carlin but was hooked clear.

Cameron rightly claimed that the ball had crossed the line but his protests fell on deaf ears and he was denied what he considered the best goal of his career.

"I'm gutted. It was the best goal I've ever scored and it was definitely over the line. I had my back to goal and put it away - I haven't even scored one like that in training," moaned Cameron.

But in the eighth minute Richard Prokas crossed from the right, Cameron flicked on in the danger area and Stevens knocked back for Baldacchino to blast his first Gretna goal low into the net from close range.

Cameron almost added to his 12 goal haul again in the 36th minute as he took down a Lee Maddison cross and let fly with a swerving 15-yard volley that slapped back off the diving Carlin's gloves.

And just before half time the in-form Gavin Skelton nutmegged Bryan Gilfillan and charged down the left to cross for Stevens who fired just wide at the near post.

The Blue Brazil stepped up a gear in the second half and Gary Fusco squandered a great chance when he fired over from a good position.

And Gretna had keeper Dave Mathieson to thank for a point blank save from a Gilfillan rocket shot.

An Ian Mauchlen corner fell at the feet of Gilfillan just eight yards out and as he blasted goalwards, Mathieson arched backwards to beat away spectacularly.

"The first twenty minutes were exceptional but we couldn't sustain that level of pressure," said Gretna gaffer Rowan Alexander.

"We ground out the result and showed good character. We made a lethargic start to the second half and caused our own problems rather than them causing us problems."

Motherwell boss and former England legend Terry Butcher watched the game from the stand.

Gretna gained another three valuable points in the promotion chase with a disciplined performance against runaway league-leaders Stirling that saw them win 1-0 at Forthbank.

Yet again, a by now customary early strike proved sufficient to secure victory. After eleven minutes Ryan Baldacchino broke down the right and fired in a low cross which Ian Stevens slid under Stirling keeper Miles Hogarth.

The home side forced several corners which were easily mopped up by the Gretna defence and David Mathieson easily dealt with anything that got through.

Gretna looked to have snatched a second goal just four minutes after the break when Hogarth could only punch out a Mick Galloway corner as far as Gavin Skelton whose shot was turned in by Stevens, but the assistants' flag was raised for offside.

Stirling made three substitutions as they tried to salvage the game but Gretna's defence held firm and restricted the home attack to long-range efforts, which were woefully off the mark. In a match that was always going to be competitive, referee Brines seemed intent on penalising any form of physical contact by Gretna players.

Pacy, livewire young striker Gary Cohen was held in the highest regard by Gretna's experienced centre-back David Holdsworth.

The 19-year-old Londoner began his career at Watford, where Holdsworth enjoyed such a successful time, before they linked up together at Scarborough in the Conference the previous season.

"David was a big influence in me coming to Gretna, definitely," said Cohen.

"He was the one that got me into Scarborough in the first place and then he asked me if I'd like to come up here as well, and I said yeah. He always tells me things that I need to improve in my game, so he's always a big help in that way."

Cohen left behind the bright neon lights and busy streets of the English capital to pursue his Gretna career and moved into a house in Carlisle.

"I don't miss London so much as my family, really. I get home a lot, but you still like to be near your family don't you," admitted the striker, who is good friends with winger Ryan Baldacchino.

"I love scoring goals. I didn't quite get into the rhythm in the first team and I'm trying to find my feet in the reserves. The Conference and the Scottish Third Division are a different kettle of fish. The Third is a lot more physical and that's what I've got to get used to - I'm slowly getting used to it."

The enthusiastic hit-man spent the early part of the season partnering Martin Cameron and said that the experience was a great addition to his football learning curve.

"Martin wins everything in the air so you've just got to read where it's going to drop down. I've watched him and he's a goalscorer, always there in the right position and I've got to learn from that."

Another legendary goalscorer that was nurturing Cohen's natural ability and honing his talent was, of course, gaffer Rowan Alexander.

"Rowan's a good boss," said Cohen. "He's pointing out things that I need to improve in my game, like hold up play that I need to improve and getting a little bit quicker so I don't get kicked as much. Everyone's helping and it's good. I'm only 19 and you never stop learning, do you?"

Cohen was aspiring to be the very best that he could, and cited some fantastic names as the players he had looked to for inspiration.

"A few years back it was Anelka because he's just an awesome striker, his pace and power, but recently it's really got to be Henry - and the Van Nistelrooy for his ability in the box."

A strangely below-par performance by Gretna saw them slump to a 2-0 defeat against a lively Montrose side.

Gretna were first to threaten with Gavin Skelton heading just over from a Ryan Baldacchino cross. At the other end David Irons rescued his side with a well-timed tackle on Craig Smart.

Montrose keeper Jim Butter did well to thwart Gavin Skelton and Ian Stevens before the home side took the lead on 40 minutes. Smart burst past Lee Maddison and crossed into the box where the ball was turned in by Roddy Black.

Gretna's misery continued three minutes later when Smart was impeded by David Irons as he closed in on goal. The veteran Gretna defender was red-carded and Scott Mitchie slammed home the spot-kick.

In the dying seconds of the half Mick Galloway saw his inswinging corner from the left hit the inside of the post and was cleared to safety.

The second half was something of an anti-climax with ten-man Gretna carrying the game to Montrose who were content to soak up the pressure and counter attack on the break.

The nearest Gretna came to scoring was when man-of-the-match Gavin Skelton hit the bar with a clever lob late in the game. David Mathieson denied Montrose a third when he tipped over a shot by Webster in the final minute.

Gretna romped into the Third Round of the Tennent's Scottish Cup with a five-goal blast to demolish Second Division Stenhousemuir at Raydale Park.

Hit man Ian Stevens completed a great week in which he was offered a new one year contract at the club by hitting a double to take claim a magnum of champange as man of the match.

And Gary Cohen, Gav Skelton and Ryan Baldacchino chipped in with one a piece to smash the Warriors.

Gretna began brightest and full back Mark Birch drilled in two early efforts, one bending away from the target and the other forcing keeper Willie McCulloch down quickly to smother.

But for all the Borderers neat passing moves and probing, when the opener came in the 37th minute it was route one.

Keeper David Mathieson pumped a long kick down the park and veteran striker Stevens got between defenders Ronnie McQuilter and Gerard McKenna and fired low inside the near post.

The Warriors had their first real sighting of goal just after the break when James McKenzie broke through the Gretna defence but blasted well over the bar from a good position and in the 51st minute Mathieson did well to turn Andrew Brown's point blank header over the bar.

Three minutes later Paul Bonar played in Martin Harty whose 18-yard drive was parried out by Mathieson but Brown was on hand to lash the rebound into the net for the leveller.

But within sixty seconds Gretna were back in front.

Gary Cohen went around McCulloch and squared from Stevens to knock in his second from close range.

McKenzie was unlucky not to level nine minutes later when Gretna failed to clear a corner and his 20-yard volley thumped back off the crossbar.

Gretna put the game beyond Stenny's reach in the 70th minute when Ryan Baldacchino crossed from the right and Cohen, running away from goal, span cleverly and drilled a low shot into the bottom corner.

Seven minutes later the pacy young striker broke into the box and unselfishly squared for Stevens, whose shot was saved by the sprawling McCulloch's feet. Mick Galloway fired the rebound back into the danger area and Gavin Skelton stretched out a leg to guide number four into the net.

Within five minutes the visitors had been reduced to nine men as their discipline went out of the window and both Bonar and McKenzie were shown red.

Baldacchino completed the rout with three minutes to play when he collected a short corner and drove home a deflected shot from the angle of the box. The winger completed his loan deal from Carlisle and put pen to paper on a three-and-a-half year deal later that week.

And on the Saturday veteran goal ace Ian Stevens showed the cool head of a ruthless assassin as he slotted in a late winner to fire Gretna back into third spot with a 2-1 victory over East Stirling.

The win takes the Borderers to within three points of promotion rivals Stranraer, who they face in a showdown next week.

Stevens pounced with just 13 minutes remaining to guide a low shot past advancing keeper Jon Connolly and into the corner of the net from 10 yards.

But the sluggish Borderers had goalkeeper Davie Mathieson to thank for a vital penalty save as basement boys 'Shire almost caused a major upset.

"These games can be a banana skin for you and the lads were very professional in getting the result," admitted Gretna boss Rowan Alexander.

"The turning point was Dave Mathieson's penalty save but I couldn't believe the decision and no-one in the ground could say that was a penalty - the lad just fell in front of David Holdsworth. It's three points at the end of the day."

Stevens had a great chance to open the scoring in the 11th minute when Gavin Skelton sent him clear, but the striker delayed his shot and keeper Connolly blocked with his feet.

Just two minutes later, 'Shire almost took a shock lead when dangerman Chris Baldwin beat Mathieson with a curling 20 yard shot that rattled the underside of the bar.

And Baldwin stretched but just couldn't get a touch on Jamie McKay's bending free kick with the goal gaping and the Gretna defence playing statues.

Gretna got back in it and midfield scrapper Richard Prokas headed on for Stevens to spin a defender and volley just wide. Ten minutes before the break the former Carlisle hit man came even closer as he got a flick on Holdsworth's powerful header, but Baldwin cleared off the line with Connolly sprawling.

The Black and Whites started purposefully after half time and Connolly had to make two diving saves to deny Gary Cohen before Raydale Park breathed a huge sigh of relief in the 51st minute as supersub Wayne Gordon hit the opener.

'Shire failed to deal with a Mick Galloway corner and Gordon's 12-yard shot through a crowd of players crashed down off the underside of the bar and up into the roof of the net.

But any Gretna hopes of the visitors rolling over were dashed as Stuart Kelly went over under a soft Holdsworth challenge and the referee pointed to the spot to general amazement.

Kelly picked himself up to take the kick, but went for placement over power and Mathieson blocked with his legs.

The visitors levelled in the 70th minute when McKay curled in another free kick and Kelly atoned for his miss by bundling into the net through a mass of bodies at the far post.

Six minutes later Stevens had his head in his hands as he controlled and fired Cohen's centre inches past the post - but within sixty seconds he beat the offside trap and his clinical finish had him celebrating his 8th strike in 11 games.

At the other end of the pitch, defender David Irons was such a massive presence in the Gretna back-line that he was dubbed 'the Rock' by fans.

He quit his job as a college lecturer in the September to sign a two-year full-time contract at the club. At 42, he was the oldest pro in the Scottish League.

Irons won the player of the season award at Raydale in 2002/03 and dropped back from his central midfield berth to a central defensive position; a move made by some of the games' greats like Franz Beckenbauer. And if he could have his career again, he said that he'd probably wish he'd started at the back.

"The move has certainly helped me extend my career," said soft-spoken Irons.

"The first time I changed position was when I was playing for Partick Thistle. I moved back in the Premier League, thoroughly enjoyed it and got a bit of recognition playing in there. To be honest, it's easier playing in there because the game's in front of you most of the time. You don't have to do quite as much running as in midfield and that's probably helped to enable me to play at the age I'm playing at," he admitted.

The vastly-experienced Irons had played for Ayr United, Clydebank, Dunfermline and St. Johnstone as well as the Jags and was snapped up by Rowan Alexander in 2001 from Annan Athletic, where he had enjoyed success as a player/manager.

"When I came to Gretna last season, I didn't expect to be playing full-time and involved in the coaching side of things, so I'm just thoroughly enjoying it. As far as the job at the college was concerned, it was a difficult decision – I spoke it over with my wife, and she was keen for me to do what I wanted to do. I don't think there's security in any job these days. Looking from the outside you would think a lecturer's job is quite secure, but they were going through a restructure and people were getting laid-off. I wasn't under any threat, but when the opportunity to get involved with Gretna FC full-time came up, it was very difficult to knock back. I've always been keen to get involved in football again on a full-time basis and I thought if I knock this back I'll probably never get another chance so I spoke it over with Rowan and Brooks, and here I am."

Irons was impressed with the buzz around Raydale and said: "I've played with some good players in some good teams, won promotion a couple of times and played a lot of Premier League football as well, which was a great experience and exciting times. But that's in the past and at the moment what Gretna are doing is very exciting. We're in a position to push on now and, fingers crossed, we'll be in the top two come May."

Irons was struck by the pace of change at the club and said that he never expected the side to get to the present level as quickly. He formed a formidable partnership with David Holdsworth at the heart of the defence, as well as the pair posing a considerable threat in the opposition box on set pieces.

"I can't speak highly enough of 'Reg' – he's absolutely magnificent. I think we're very fortunate to have someone like that playing with us because everybody can learn off him. He's a joy to play with and a gentleman off the park as well," said Irons, who's also been impressed by team-mates such as Gavin Skelton, Davie Mathieson, Ryan Baldacchino and Martin Cameron.

And as for being called the 'Rock'? "It makes a changes from being called Gandalf!" he joked.

"I've got a role to play in the team and I'm just trying to do it to the best of my ability. Hopefully the players round about will learn from the experienced players in the team and I'm just delighted to be given the opportunity to pass things on to the rest of the side."

Gretna came out on top 2-1 in a dour local derby with Stranraer and at the same time drew level on points with their second-placed hosts. A heavy pitch was not conductive to the Raydale sides' fluent football but when it came to grinding out a result, Rowan Alexander's men were certainly not found wanting. After a tentative opening twenty minutes by both sides, Lee Sharp broke clear of the Gretna defence but was denied by David Mathieson, then David Graham flashed a shot across the Gretna goal.

The opening goal and indeed the only highlight of a dreary first-half came after 31 minutes when Mark Birch fired in an unstoppable 40-yard drive that whistled past keeper Andy McCondichie and into the top corner of the net.

Stranraer came out after the break with all guns blazing and on 50 minutes Mathieson did well to tip over a header by hot-shot Michael Moore. A minute later the Stranraer striker was celebrating when he headed in a Sharp cross for the equaliser.

Gretna rallied and on 62 minutes Ryan Baldacchino broke clear but was foiled by a brave dive by McCondichie. The winner came after 76 minutes when Birch's cross from the right was only cleared as far as Mick Galloway. The Gretna skipper fired home a scorching left-footer from the edge of the box.

Gretna defended comfortably for the remainder of the game as the home side appeared to have run out of ideas.

The club crashed out of the Tennent's SFA Cup 3-0 at Clyde and in the league new signing Derek Townsley watched on from the stand as a late Steven Reilly header rocked Raydale with Queen's Park winning 1-0.

The former Hibs, Motherwell, Carlisle and Oxford star was probably amazed as to how his new team-mates failed to register as the woodwork twice came to Queen's rescue.

But the Spiders could have added more themselves but for the agility and positional sense of keeper Dave Mathieson as the pacy, hard-working front line of Derek Carcary, Frankie Carroll and Paul Harvey caused problems.

As early as the third minute Carcary broke down the left and fired in a fierce shot that Mathieson dived to block.

Two minutes later at the other end Ross Clark cleared a dangerous Ryan Baldacchino centre from under his own crossbar as Gary Cohen stretched but just couldn't reach with his head.

Baldacchino was on fire, jinking past three and four men at will, and as he embarked on a great solo run he was clipped down on the edge of the box by Damiano Agostini. Gavin Skelton's resultant free kick was drilled past the wall but deflected just wide.

In the 12th minute Lee Maddison lost out to John Whelan who crossed and Carroll guided a side-footed volley straight into the grateful Mathieson's arms from 8 yards when he should have scored.

Gretna hit back and Mick Galloway sprayed a brilliant long ball to release Ian Stevens down the left, but as he cut into the danger area he dragged his low shot past the near post.

Within two minutes Carcary's good work down the right created an opening for Stevie Fallon but his deflected shot was brilliantly tipped around the post by the full stretch Mathieson.

On the half hour Baldacchino burst into the Queen's box and angled a shot towards the top corner that was acrobatically turned over by keeper Derek Scrimgour. Baldacchino whipped in the resultant corner and David Holdsworth was unlucky to see his powerful header rattle the bar.

Then Gavin Skelton had the crowd on their feet as he curled a 20-yarder inches past the upright with Scrimgour well beaten.

Cohen got into the box a couple of minutes later and squared low for strike-partner Stevens who will be having nightmares as he blasted over from 4 yards with the empty net at his mercy.

And right on half time Cohen drilled in another low centre that rattled off Agostini's shins and crashed back off his own post.

After an action packed first period there were little fireworks after the break. Holdsworth showed a cool head as he cleared off the line from Carroll and Scrimgour was forced to turn a stinging Mark Birch long range free kick over the top.

Gaffer Rowan Alexander introduced top-gun Martin Cameron, Danny Lennon and 'Buzzer' Gordon as Gretna went in search of a winner.

But with the game looking destined for an unlikely goal-less draw, just two minutes from time the Spiders swung in a corner from the right and Reilly rose unchallenged to thump a header into the bottom corner of the net through a crowd of players.

But Gretna bounced back and sent out a powerful message to their title rivals when they returned to form with a 2-1 win at Cowdenbeath.

A deflected strike from captain Mick Galloway settled a tense contest and inflicted a harsh blow on Cowden's own promotion hopes.

The home side had the ball in the net after 35 minutes when Gretna old boy Steve Skinner crossed for Dene Shields to net but the goal was chalked out for offside.

Gretna grabbed the lead in the 39th minute when striker Ian Stevens hit his ninth goal of the season.

Galloway's corner was headed home by his former Carlisle United team-mate.

But two minutes later the Blue Brazil levelled when the Gretna defence failed to get to grips with Skinner, who broke through and fired home from 15 yards.

With the game evenly balanced, Gretna keeper Davie Mathieson saved his side when Innes Richie's header was parried on the line.

There was just 10 minutes remaining when Galloway's 30-yard drive took a deflection that left Cowden keeper Andy Carlin stranded.

Gretna hit-man Martin Cameron was on the road for 80 minutes during his daily drive to Raydale from his home in Penicuik.

And the 25-year-old striker was hoping to get back in the driving seat on the pitch by reclaiming his number 9 shirt after spending a month hampered by a thigh injury.

Cameron limped off during Gretna's 1-0 victory at Stirling on the 6th December.

"It's been frustrating – it's been six weeks now and I'm just getting back into it. I would have been back a lot sooner but obviously I was in hospital over the New Year for a week with an illness, so it's been longer than I anticipated," said Cameron.

A few eyebrows were raised when Cameron moved from the First Division to join Gretna, but the striker had no doubts whatsoever that he had made the right decision in making the move to the Borders.

"It's taken time for the club to get used to being full-time, but you can see on the park that we're getting results and we're getting there. I'm enjoying it and I'm dying to get back into the first team – hopefully sooner rather than later."

"I've played in the Third Division before, so I know what it's all about. It's a hard league to get out of and it's going to be hard for us to catch the two above us, but we have the faith that we can do it."

Cameron said he doesn't set himself any goalscoring targets. "I just go out there and score as many goals as I can – the more I get, obviously, the better, but I never set myself targets because that sets you up for a fall. I'm disappointed because I've only got 12 – at this stage last season I had 19, and that was in the First Division. But I've missed few games and that hasn't helped so I'm dying to get back in and finish as high as I can in the goalscoring charts."

He made his comeback in a 1-1 draw at Elgin with squalls of driving snow putting the match in doubt until referee Alan Freeland's requirements for red painted lines and a yellow ball were met and the snow abated.

Playing into the wind Gretna started well with debutant Derek Townsley comfortable in defence in the absence of the suspended David Holdsworth. Ryan Baldacchino's pace and control had the home defence at panic stations. In the 12th minute Martin Cameron met his cross to shoot cleanly past home keeper Pirie, but a dubious offside decision ruled it out.

Five minutes later Ian Stevens went clean through but another offside ruling went against the visitors. Gretna got the break-through their pressure deserved from another Baldacchino-Cameron combination. Baldacchino outpaced the left side defence and crossed to Cameron. Pirie could only parry his shot and the winger followed up to power a shot into the bottom right corner. Gretna dominated but the only clear chance ended with Mick Galloway shooting over after Cameron and Gavin Skelton's build up.

Elgin played well from the restart but on the hour Gretna were in control again. In the 61st Skelton crossed pinpoint to Cameron but his header was too straight at Pirie. The big striker turned provider six minutes later, beating three men in a mazy run from the bye-line on the left only for Stevens to shoot narrowly wide from his pass. In the 69th Cameron headed just over the bar.

With five minutes left Gretna drove for the second goal that would make the game safe. David Irons met Galloway's inswinging free-kick perfectly to head just wide. In the next move Skelton shot just over the bar from 30 yards and the visitors last chance in the 88th was a repetition of an Irons' near miss from Galloway's free-kick.

Elgin now sensed the chance of snatching a point. Mathieson deflected Alex Bone's shot brilliantly in the 90th. The home team's man-of-the-match Craig Tully then powered McKenzie's free-kick past Mathieson and in off the post for a real kick in the teeth.

Gretna midfielder Derek Townsley was 'chuffed' as he marked his return to Raydale with a home debut goal in a 3-0 victory over Albion Rovers. The 6'5" former Hibs and Motherwell ace said: " It brought back a lot of memories - I thoroughly enjoyed it and to get a goal just capped it off."

Gretna stormed in front in the second minute when Mick Galloway played a quick short corner to Ryan Baldacchino whose centre was powerfully headed home by top-gun Martin

Cameron. Rovers almost levelled in the 21st minute, but keeper Dave Mathieson brilliantly turned Tony Low's drive over the bar at full-stretch - and 8 minutes later the Borderers made them pay.

Danny Lennon, making his full debut in a Gretna shirt having been hampered by injury since signing from Partick in the Summer, knocked a great ball into Ian Stevens. The veteran striker span and fired into the bottom corner, wrong footing keeper Neil Bennett.

Baldacchino was proving a constant threat and in the 39th minute he jinked into the Rovers box and squared into the path of Townsley who swept home the third.

Paul McManus nearly got a consolation just after the break but his header rattled the bar.

Townsley was denied a second when Bennett parried out his close range header and Baldacchino also forced the keeper into a full stretch save.

Former Carlisle postman Townsley felt he could have had an even greater impact on the game.

"The gaffer wanted me to get in the box because he wants to get more goals from midfield and, to be fair, I could have had a hat-trick," he told the reporters after the game.

"It was great to be back playing at Raydale Park again. My parents were in the stand and it was a bit strange for them seeing me back," he said, wearing a smart grey club suit and a pair of stylish glasses.

"I'm versatile and, as long as I'm playing, I don't care if I'm at the back, in midfield or up front. In the past it has worked against me but I enjoy being able to play in different positions," said Townsley, who signed a three-and a-half year deal after returning North from Oxford United.

"I'm just pleased to be playing again for people I have a lot of respect for like Brooks Mileson and the gaffer."

Cameron hit another hat-trick in a 4-2 win at East Stirling with skipper Mick Galloway adding the other but Montrose striker Craig Smart then put a massive dent in Gretna's promotion hopes as he hit a second half double. The Gable Endies pulled off a smash-and-grab raid as they came back from a goal behind to send the Borderers crashing to their third home defeat of the season. Goal- hero Smart said: "We battled away well and took our chances."

Gretna hit man Martin Cameron fired the black-and-whites in front in the 6th minute. Derek Townsley played a clever ball over the top and Cameron showed great composure as he volleyed over advancing keeper Jim Butter and into the roof of the net for his 17th goal of the season.

His strike partner Ian Stevens could have made it two six minutes later but shot wide after Butter had parried a Cameron header.

But Montrose saw Kevin Webster, Steve Kerrigan and Smart all go close before the break. And Smart levelled in the 51st minute when Gretna suffered a mix-up at the back and Webster crossed for him to guide into the corner from close range.

He was on hand again in the 74th minute when Lee Maddison left a back pass short and Martin Wood nipped in to fire against Dave Mathieson - with Smart following up to net the rebound.

The Third Division promotion race reached boiling point at Raydale Park as Gretna hit man Brian Wake fired a dream debut strike and referee Cammy Melville brandished 12 cards - including THREE red in a 1-0 win over rivals Stirling.

Wake, who had been plagued by injury since arriving at the club from Carlisle in December, was desperately unlucky not to open his account in the eighth minute. Ryan Baldacchino whipped in a centre and Wake's glancing header was brilliantly tipped away by Albion keeper Myles Hogarth at full stretch.

League leaders Stirling suffered a blow in the 12th minute when former Celtic ace Mark McNally was stretchered off after a goalmouth scramble.

Tempers flared in the 27th minute as Gretna's Gavin Skelton and Baldacchinno and Stirling's Paul Nugent went in the book following a Skelton foul.

Five minutes later skipper Mick Galloway cleverly knocked a Baldacchino centre into the path of Wake who sidefooted into the corner of the net from close range with the Binos defence playing statues.

Albion were rocked again six minutes later as Derek

Anderson was shown red for a wild lunge at his tormentor Baldacchino. But ref Melville evened things up within two minutes when he dismissed David Holdsworth for allegedly retaliating to a foul from striker Ryan Davidson.

The Binos were reduced to nine men six minutes after the break when Paul Nugent was shown a second yellow for taking down Martin Cameron on the edge of the box.

Cameron was unlucky not to make it two when Richard Prokas chased a lost cause and played back to Gavin Skelton whose curling cross was met by the 17-goal striker, his powerful header rattling the bar.

Gretna keeper Dave Mathieson pulled off a stunning fingertip save to keep out Derek Lyle in the dying seconds and the Black and White's hearts were in the mouths as the resultant corner was headed inches over the bar.

Gretna couldn't build on the success and two quick-fire goals twelve minutes from time left the Borderers pointless and facing a high, high mountain to climb in the hunt for promotion as they went down 2-1 at Peterhead.

Gretna began well with Mick Galloway prominent in midfield and Ryan Baldacchino's ball control and pace stretching the home defence to the limit as he alternated between left and right flanks.

The first good chance came though at the other end as David Mathieson cleared Peterhead's first corner at the second attempt.

Gretna went ahead in the 27th minute. Baldacchino was fouled on the left. He took the kick himself and placed it perfectly for Derek Townsley to rise and power an unstoppable header past home keeper Mathers.

Gretna were in control and in the 33rd minute Ryan McGuffie shot well but too straight at Mathers and in the 41st another Townsley header from Galloway's free kick was just wide.

On the stroke of half time Bavidge just failed to turn Roddie's low cross in for Peterhead's best chance.

Gretna kept up their midfield dominance into the second half. On the hour three corners in succession ended with Ian Stevens' effort coming back off the post.

Disaster struck in the 77th and 79th minutes. First a Townsley back-header dropped short and Andy Roddie burst through to shoot past Mathieson from six yards. The roof fell in on Gretna's afternoon when Peterhead took a free-kick with the referee's whistle awaited. Midfielder Jamie Buchan played a fast one-two with Roddie and fired home from the left-side of the goal.

Gretna were now desperate to salvage a point. A Mick Galloway free-kick was deflected out in the 89th minute. Derek Townsley met the corner for a last chance header but it went narrowly wide and so it was a long journey home with no reward for the good football played.

Gretna midfielder Gavin Skelton couldn't believe it as he fired in a swerving, dipping 20-yard drive that left Stranraer keeper Andy McCondichie rooted to the spot but smashed off the crossbar in a must-win game at Raydale.

It was tough luck on both the hard-working former Carlisle and Workington ace, who was at the heart of the Borderers best moves, and on gaffer Rowan Alexander who had seen his team dominate.

A blank scoresheet was probably the last result on anyone's mind in a game containing the Third Division's top guns - Blues' Michael Moore and Gretna's Martin Cameron - who have netted 39 times between them this season.

A point suited second-placed Stranraer more than their Dumfries and Galloway rivals, and they remained nine points clear with nine games to play.

But boss Alexander wasn't too downbeat and said: "We had to win but there's still a lot of football to be played. We had at least six chances in the first half but we lacked a cutting edge in front of goal and it's been the same story all season. I wasn't disappointed with the way we played. We adopted a system with just Cammy up front that caused them problems and I felt that we dominated the game."

Brian Wake was first to test McCondichie when he drilled in a low shot that the keeper dived to smother at the near post.

And soon after Wake teed up skipper Mick Galloway who flashed a drive wide. Just four minutes later, Cameron headed back for inrushing full-back Ryan McGuffie who hit a sweet volley from 18 yards that zipped inches past the post.

Skelton began pulling the strings and was instrumental in setting up chances for Wake, Cameron and Ryan Baldacchino who all went close in a five-minute spell.

Gretna target Moore looked out of sorts at the other end with his strike partner David Graham posing a much greater threat on the break.

On the half hour he fired in a cross that flicked off Davie Irons head and full-back Stephen Swift chested down and hammered in a volley that keeper Dave Mathieson brilliantly tipped over the bar.

Five minutes later Graham cut in from the right and unleashed a fierce angled drive that bent inches wide.

Stranraer lost their attacking impetus after the break when Swift was replaced by Christopher Cruickshank and the Black and Whites were camped in their half.

In the 63rd minute Baldacchino received a quick corner from Galloway and Wake met his cross on the volley, only for his goalbound shot to be deflected out from a body in the packed six yard box.

And when Skelton's drive left the bar vibrating and thumped out four minutes later, it just wasn't going to be Gretna's day.

Stranraer almost stole an unlikely win late on when Leigh Collins drilled a low cross into the box that found sub Cruickshank unmarked at the back post, but Mathieson produced a superb block to keep out his powerful drive.

Two thunderbolt strikes from defenders Lee Maddison and David Irons grabbed the three points to keep Gretna's promotion push on track with a 2-1 win over Elgin.

But the Black and Whites were giving an early fright as second-bottom City took a shock lead in a game marred by a swirling wind and heavy showers.

In the seventh minute, City's Willie Martin fired in a cross from the right and as full-back Ryan McGuffie chested down in an attempt to clear the difficult ball, Kevin Steele nipped in to poke off his toes and past keeper Dave Mathieson from 14 yards.

But Gretna's response was instant - and brilliant. Lee Maddison picked up the ball fully 30-yards from goal and let fly with an unstoppable low drive that flew past keeper Martin Pirie and crashed into the corner of the net off the foot of the post.

McGuffie attempted to atone for his error when he drove in a 30-yarder that Pirie dived to block and the keeper had to be on his toes again just minutes later as Gavin Skelton cracked in a shot.

City were reduced to ten men in the 33rd minute when Hugh Dickson received his marching orders for a foul on Richard Prokas.

And Gretna went in front four minutes before the break when Galloway turned the City defence inside out and teed-up Irons who hammered home from 30-yards.

Gretna dominated the second half and almost added a third when sub Gary Cohen's shot came back off the woodwork.

With the two sides above them failing to win, Gretna's promotion hopes in the Bell's Scottish League Division Three received a fillip with a 2-1 victory at Albion Rovers.

They scored a seventh-minute goal when Derek Townsley's centre was only half cleared and Ryan Baldacchino slammed the ball into the net from 15 yards.

Inspired by this, Gretna dominated and Albion goalkeeper Neil Bennett had to be at his best to save from Gavin Skelton.

The visitors lost Martin Cameron but the reorganisation did not deter them and substitute Ian Stevens put his side two up.

When the home defence hesitated, Stevens unleashed a 30-yard effort which flashed past keeper Bennett.

Albion retaliated and after David Mathieson pulled off an excellent save from Jim Mercer, the home side cut the deficit. A corner by Jed Stirling was headed past his own keeper by Stevens.

The second half was drab and although Albion had a lot of possession it rarely looked like penetrating the Gretna defence for a second time. Indeed, it was the promotion challengers who almost scored again but Gary Cohen was robbed at the last second by Shaun Sweeney.

Gretna took another step towards their dream of promotion to the Bell's Scottish League Division Two with a 1-0 victory at Stirling Albion, who began the day in pole position.

An only goal means Gretna are just five points adrift of Stirling as the battle for the two promotion places heated up.

Stirling dominated the opening exchanges, with Craig Ferguson and Derek Lyle going close, but the visitors gradually came more into the picture and took the lead in the 26th minute.

Lee Maddison pin-pointed a cross from the left, which Derek Townsley headed home.

There could have been a second seven minutes later, as an effort from Gary Cohen rebounded from the upright.

Early in the second half Ian Stevens broke clear, but after rounding the goalkeeper he fired his shot against the crossbar.

Stirling were far from out of it though, and Gretna's goalkeeper David Mathieson was called upon to make excellent saves from Lyle and Stuart Divine.

Towards the end, Mathieson had to fingertip over the top a goalbound effort from Gary Kelly, and at the opposite end home goalkeeper Miles Hogarth did well to turn away a Lee Maddison header.

With just seconds remaining, Stirling were unlucky when David O'Brien headed against the post.

But Gretna held on for a crucial and well-deserved victory.

Hopes were high when Cowdenbeath visited Raydale but Gaffer Rowan Alexander said his players were left numb in the dressing room after Bryan Gilfillan netted to complete a smash-and-grab raid.

The Borderers promotion hopes took a massive blow as John McKeown pumped a ball into the box and Gilfillan crashed a volley into the roof of the net in the 70th minute.

"It was flat - no atmosphere in the ground," said Alexander.

"We knew they'd be hard to break down but we created plenty of chances. There's still 15 points to play for and we never say die. It's made it difficult losing today and our home record has killed us really."

Gretna almost got off to a dream start but Cowden keeper Andy Carlin made a super save from Dave Irons' header.

Lee Maddison then flashed a long range drive inches past the post before Carlin again did well to parry out a Derek Townsley header and smother Ian Stevens' follow up in the 32nd minute.

Gretna had the Cowden half under siege in the second half and Ryan Baldacchino and sub Brian Wake both went close with powerful efforts before Gilfillan rocked Raydale.

Townsley had two headers deflected away in a packed box and Gretna piled on the pressure, but Cowden sub John Paul Kelly almost added a breakaway second when he raced through and lobbed the advancing Dave Mathieson, his shot going just wide.

Wake had a penalty appeal waved away before being shown a second yellow card in the dying seconds.

Former Hibs & Motherwell ace Derek Townsley hit a hat-trick to sink East Stirling 5-1 - and admitted afterwards he hadn't claimed the matchball because he felt his second goal was 'iffy.'

Townsley was deployed as a target man by Gretna boss Rowan Alexander and said: "I spoke about playing striker with the gaffer through the week. I've played everywhere bar goalkeeper now. I haven't taken the matchball because my second goal was iffy - I know a proper striker would have claimed it, but I'm an honest lad."

'Shire hit the self-destruct bottom in the 5th minute when Richard Prokas curled in a centre that Ryan Baldacchino headed back and unlucky defender Graham McGhee looped a header into his own net.

The basement club could have levelled when Derek Ure split the Gretna defence but Scott Livingstone shot against Dave Mathieson's legs. Paul Rodden rose unmarked at the back post from the resultant corner, but Mathieson got down quickly to save.

And sixty seconds later it was 2-0 when Ian Stevens beat outrushing keeper Chris Todd to a long ball and fired across him into the net.

Townsley made it three in the 40th minute with a towering header that crashed in off the underside of the bar.

'Shire pulled one back on the hour as Ure drilled over a low centre and Darren Millar struck sweetly into the bottom corner.

But Townsley struck again 13 minutes from time, firing home a cross from sub Wayne Gordon and he headed in his treble from close range off a Mark Eccles corner right on time.

Big Townsley then hit a double with Brian Wake also adding two as the club romped to a 4-1 win at bogey side Montrose.

Gretna had taken just one point off the Gable Endies in their previous three encounters - but any fears that the Raydale outfit may have had were blown away after just six minutes when Townsley nodded on a corner and Wake headed into the net for the opener.

Townsley rose to head in a Gavin Skelton corner for 2-0 in the 40th minute and set up Wake to fire in the third just two minutes after the break.

Martin Wood pulled one back just after the hour but Townsley completed the rout in the 84th minute with another header.

Gretna's outside chance of promotion faded away in the bright sunshine of Stair Park won 3-2 ensuring their prompt return to the SFL 2nd Division - almost certainly as 3rd Division Champions.

Stranraer made their attacking intent plain from the kick-off with David Mathieson having to parry David Graham's snap shot to safety in the 3rd minute. Ryan Baldacchino threatened briefly but Stranraer swept upfield again and Mathieson had to be quick to cut out a dangerous cross from Kevin Finlayson and save another stinger from Graham.

With fifteen minutes played Gretna attacked in strength. Balacchino's run was checked at the expense of a corner. Gavin Skelton's inswinger caught the defence out and Derek Townsley rose to head cleanly past McCondichie in the 17th minute.

Straight from the kick-off Stranraer forced three corners in quick succession - the second forcing a superb Mathieson save from home skipper Jenkins. From the third David Turnbull, deputising for suspended hitman Michael Moore, headed in an excellent first goal for his club.

Apart from a long-range Mark Birch effort and a blocked Ian Stevens shot Gretna were on the back foot but defended well until half-time.

Stranraer began the second half with the same thrust as they had the first. In the 48th minute Graham won possesion on the right, cut in diagonally and hit a swerving, deflected shot past Mathieson. Gretna skipper Davie Irons was adamant that

Graham had fouled Ryan McGuffie on his run in. Referee Mack would have none of it and booked not only Irons but Mathieson and Townsley too for their protests.

Townsley continued to be Gretna's main threat and the midfield looked more lively with Galloway on for Baldacchino in the 62nd. Birch tried again but didn't trouble McCondichie.

In the 65th Stranraer went two up. Graham brought down defender Fraser Wright's 60-yard clearance in one move, spotted Mathieson coming out and lobbed him perfectly from the edge of the box in the next.

The Stranraer fans' celebrations began but Gretna would not be spring lambs to the slaughter and Galloway led the fight back.

With 5 minutes to go Murray Henderson handled on the line and Brian Wake converted the penalty.

In the 88th minute Townsley met Wake's cross out jumping his marker and heading firmly clear of McCondichie but just over the bar and as the final whistle blew the home management and players ran to celebrate with their jubilant fans.

A 3-2 win over Peterhead saw Gretna hold on to claim third spot - but they were made to sweat after the Blue Toon staged a second half fightback in a thriller at Raydale.

The Borderers got off to an explosive start and almost opened the scoring in the first minute when Derek Townsley pulled back to Gavin Skelton whose fierce low shot was parried wide by keeper Paul Mathers.

Gretna were sweeping the ball around the pitch with great confidence and in the 13th minute skipper Mick Galloway floated a delightful ball out to Skelton who fired in a first time cross that the inrushing Ian Stevens rifled against the woodwork.

Ryan Baldacchino was tormenting Peterhead full back Shaun McSkimming with his tricky running and six minutes later he got into the box and pulled a dangerous ball back to Stevens whose low shot was cleared off the line by Robbie Raeside.

Gretna's industry and inventiveness earned themselves the opener in the 23rd minute - and it was an absolute cracker.

There looked little danger when Jamie Buchan fouled Lee

Maddison 30 yards from goal, but Galloway teed up Mark Birch who sent an absolute screamer whistling into the net.

Four minutes later Peterhead had their first sight of goal but Dave Mathieson brilliantly turned over Martin Bavidge's fiercely struck volley one handed.

And in the 33rd minute Baldacchino jinked past two defenders and curled a fantastic solo effort over Mathers and looping into the top corner for number two.

Some of Gretna's attacking play was breathtaking and just two minutes later Stevens played a great one-two with Skelton whose clever back-heel sent the veteran hit-man clear to slot low into the net.

Just seconds after the break Gretna almost grabbed a fourth when Mathers spilled a Baldacchino cross under pressure from Townsley, but Skelton sliced his volley inches over the bar.

Peterhead pulled one back in the 49th minute when Bavidge crossed to the far post and Raeside powered home a header.

And Gretna were stunned sixty seconds later when Kris Brash drifted in a corner that Raeside headed back and Bavidge applied the finish touch, nodding in from close range.

Nine minutes later Gretna's hearts were in their mouths when Bavidge almost levelled as he held off two challenges on the edge of the box but his low drive came back off the post.

Sub Gary Cohen came close to sealing it for Gretna late on when his pace and determined running took him past Raeside but his shot was dragged and Mathers smothered comfortably.

Despite having first use of a new pitch installed for the Cup Final at Hampden Park the following week, Queen's Park and Gretna served up a typical end of season encounter with a 1-1 draw to end the campaign.

Rowan Alexander rang the changes bringing in young keeper Craig Summersgill, defender Kyle May and midfielder Colin Spence for their first games of the season. All performed creditably.

The home side hit the bar in the 10th minute courtesy of a David McCallum volley from the edge of the box.

Four minutes later the Queen's crossbar denied Colin Spence from 25 yards. Gretna came close again with good efforts from Mark Eccles and Derek Townsley clearing the bar.

Queen's took the lead in the 35th minute when McCallum's shot from the edge of the box appeared to take a deflection past Summersgill. In the final seconds of the first half the young Gretna keeper saved his side when he blocked a shot from Derek Carcary.

In the opening minutes of the second half Whelan blasted over the bar for the home side before substitute Brian Wake just failed to get on the end of a Mark Eccles cross for Gretna. The home side could have increased their lead in the 70th minute when good build-up saw Frankie Carroll in the clear but he blazed the ball over the bar with only Summersgill to beat.

Scoring chances were at a premium but Mick Galloway almost grabbed the equaliser but saw his 20-yard effort deflected for a corner.

When it looked as if time was running out for the equaliser Gretna's play deserved, Brian Wake rose above the home defence to head home Ryan Baldacchino's cross from the right with just three minutes left on the clock.

With Montrose notching a late winner at Peterhead, Gretna consolidated their third place finish - seven points ahead of the north-east side with a 68 point total.

Three
Season 2004/05
Third Division Champions

THERE was shock news over the summer break as popular 31-year-old defender Lee Maddison was diagnosed with non-Hodgkin's lymphoma - a mild form of leukaemia. Good will messages poured into the club from all over the country for Maddison, who received chemotherapy at Newcastle's RVI hospital.

After a visit to see Lee on the ward, Managing Director Brooks Mileson said: "Lee is in very good spirits and is feeling very positive about what's happening. He is full of resolve that he's going to get back and is absolutely determined to play again, which is a great thing. He is really perky and pleased with his treatment. He is joking about it, which is typical Maddy."

Skipper Mick Galloway added: "It's unbelievable how much we miss him with his big laugh and his jokes. There's a gap in the dressing room."

Gretna signed towering striker and qualified Doctor Kenny Deuchar from East Fife, experienced former Falkirk, Aberdeen, Hibs, Dundee United and Celtic defender Jamie McQuilken was signed on-loan from St. Johnstone as cover for Maddison, skilful and exciting forward David Bingham from Inverness Caley Thistle, bustling, powerful hit-man Andy Smith from Clyde, goalkeeper Alan Main who had been at a number of clubs including Dundee United and St. Johnstone, and Rowan Alexander also snapped up defender Andy Aitken from neighbours Queen of the South. "Andy was one of my first signings as manager of Queen of the South in 1997. He's an experienced, loyal player who I am sure will be an ideal replacement for the retiring David Irons," he said.

The club had a pre-season training camp spending seven days surrounded by the breathtaking scenery of Northern Italy, near the Alps, in the Hotel Garda, Affi. The Italian Job was a great success. Unlike the classic Sixties movie, there were no mafia hoods in dark glasses and trilby hats waiting in the winding hills to put the motors over a cliff with an earthmover - nor was Benny Hill driving the coach - but the players boots did get nicked!

Kenny Deuchar and Ryan McGuffie scored the goals in Gretna's first-ever fixture on foreign soil as Gretna fought back from two down to draw with a Verona select side and Ryan Baldacchino, Mick Galloway and new boys David Bingham and Kenny Deuchar were on target in a 4-2 over Shanghai.

The club trained in the superb facilities used by the Italian national side at the Hotel Veronello and were made very welcome throughout the tour.

Former Manchester United, Motherwell and Clyde midfielder Stephen Cosgrove was snapped up and ex-Carlisle United midfielder Mark Boyd was also signed by the club as the rebuilding continued, turning down the glorious sunshine and beautiful ramshackle white-washed villages of Portugal to join up.

Boyd wasn't keen on struggling with a new language at Mick Wadsworth's Beira Mar side and had been set to jet out and join up after attracting the interest of a number of clubs but Gretna signed him after he impressed in a pre-season friendly against Dalbeattie Star.

At Raydale Park the pitch was widened and re-laid in a £60,000 ground redevelopment over the break and winger Ryan Baldacchino revelled in the new surface by scoring one and setting up two more for David Bingham and Andy Smith as Gretna romped to a 3-0 Bell's Challenge Cup win over Montrose. But Baldacchino said if he had his own way, the pitch would be even wider. "The pitch is bigger, which works to my advantage. But if I had a say in it I would still stretch it an extra couple of yards!" joked Baldacchino. "Teams came here and sat in against us last season so hopefully the bigger pitch will work in our favour. It was great to score a goal against Montrose as I didn't get enough last season."

On the opening day of the league campaign midfielder Stephen Cosgrove took just seven minutes to net his first senior goal after coming off the bench as the black and whites gave Albion Rovers a lesson is six education.

David Bingham hit a brilliant first half double while strike partner Andy Smith and skipper Mick Galloway both struck before late substitutes Cosgrove and Kenny Deuchar completed the onslaught.

The former Manchester United and Motherwell ace admitted: "It was brilliant to score. The closest I got to hitting the net previously was when I was with Clyde. I would have liked to know what odds I would have got to be a scorer because it was a long shot - but hopefully it was the first of many."

Fellow sub Ryan McGuffie slid a great ball into his path and Cosgrove fired low across sprawling keeper Mark Peat and into the corner of the net in the 86th minute for number five.

Gretna had an early scare when bulky striker Mark Yardley flicked on for John Bradford but he hooked his volley wide from a great position.

Gretna hit back and only a great blocking tackle by Danny Black denied Smith, then Gavin Skelton's drive stung Peat's palms.

Skelton suffered a clash of heads with Marc McKenzie on 15 minutes and with blood pouring from the wound had to leave the pitch for three stitches – but while Gretna were temporarily down to ten men, Bingham struck twice.

He stretched to guide a clever chip over the stranded Peat for the opener in the 22nd minute and three minutes later fired into the roof of the net after Smith's shot had come back off the post.

Bradley should have pulled one back in the 27th minute when Yardley's flick sent him clear, but shot tamely and David Mathieson saved low to his left.

It was one-way traffic after the break and skipper Galloway added the third on the hour when he pounced to fire home the loose ball after Peat had spilled a Ryan Baldacchino cross.

Big hit-man Smith lashed in number four from the edge of the box in the 72nd minute after the ball broke loose from a challenge on Bingham.

Deuchar immediately replaced Smith and caused the Rovers defence a new set of problems, slicing wide just seconds after coming on and then forcing a good save from Peat with a powerful downward header from a Mark Birch cross.

But he was not to be denied and in the second minute of stoppage time powerfully held off two challenges and smacked the sixth high into the corner of the net from 15 yards.

It was easy to see why boss Rowan Alexander had put David Bingham top of his summer wish list after his two-goal debut performance. "He's an absolute joy to watch," said Alexander.

Bingham, as sleek an elegant around the box as a Ferrari, had come off with a bit of tightness in his hamstring and said: "It was a fantastic team performance and nice to score four goals when we only had ten men on the pitch – that shows just how hard we worked."

"I played with Andy Smith at Dunfermline and it's nice to play with someone who you have an understanding with and are on the same wavelength as. It's been a fantastic start for us, but the worst thing we can do now is get carried away by it all. I'm certain that won't happen because there is a long season ahead of us, and the lads are professionals. We have set the standard in terms of application and work-rate and we've got to keep it going. We are not going to win 6-0 every week, but we've shown people what we are capable of."

But after such a convincing start, Gretna laboured to a 2-1 win at perennial strugglers East Stirling the following week. Bingham almost put Gretna ahead in the 33rd minute, but 'Shire keeper Ross Gilpin produced a reflex save to turn his header onto the post and away for a corner. One minute later, Gretna did go in front when Andy Aitken headed Bingham's cross from the left into the net from 15 yards.

The lead only lasted four minutes as Chris Millar curled a 20-yard free kick into David Mathieson's top left hand corner.

Gretna hit the winner four minutes before the break when Andy Smith controlled and laid back for Derek Townsley to smash home from ten yards. 'Shire sub Gordon Parks had the ball in the net in the 86th minute but was clearly offside and deep into injury time Parks was again unlucky as he saw his shot from 15 yards smash back off the crossbar.

Gretna's interest in the CIS Cup was ended in the first round when Morton sub Paul Walker struck sixteen minutes from time in a pulsating contest at Cappielow.

Walker, who had only been on the field five minutes, fired in a low drive that beat Mathieson at his right hand post. Gretna should have equalised with four minutes to go when Baldacchino's cross from the right caused panic in the home defence and both Andy Smith and Kenny Deuchar saw their efforts blocked on the line as Gretna span out.

Left-back Gavin Skelton fired in a rocket drive as Gretna maintained their unbeaten league run with a 1-0 victory over Montrose at Raydale. Ryan McGuffie rolled a neat ball into Skelton's path and he drilled a 25-yard exocet into the corner of the net just seconds after the break.

"I was delighted with the goal and it is always nice to score the winner," said Skelton, a large white bandage still on his head following his injury against Montrose on the opening day. "Most teams will try and shut us down but we must be patient and take our chances when they come. There are no easy games in this league and every team is capable of picking up points against us. With such a large squad there is a lot of competition for places, but that's good for the team as you must play your best or you're out."

Gretna had plenty of possession as they moved the ball around confidently in the first half and Andy Smith went close in the 16th minute when his glancing header from a Ryan Baldacchino corner flew just wide.

But Montrose almost grabbed a shock opener in the 29th minute when Euan Hall took down Barry Donachie's deep cross and hit a sweet half-volley onto the roof of the net. Seconds later Baldacchino broke down the left and Steve Kerrigan had to produce a brilliant blocking tackle on the line as McGuffie threatened to ram in his low centre.

Three minutes after Skelton's wonder strike Mick Galloway turned cleverly and chipped into the box for Smith to flick on and David Bingham drilled just wide.

Baldacchino was proving a constant menace down the left and on the hour he released Bingham who crossed deep for McGuffie to fire in a shot that Alan Budd blocked on the line.

Galloway lifted a shot over the bar and Skelton went close to adding a second when he fizzed another low drive inches wide from distance.

Montrose showed little up front but Craig Smart forced keeper David Mathieson into a diving save with a powerful drive in the 77th minute.

Bingham and Baldacchino combined with nine minutes to play but as the former Caley Thistle man bore down on goal, keeper Michael Hankinson stood his ground and saved his poked shot with his legs.

Gretna then went down to a shock 3-2 defeat at Hampden as Queen's Park substitute Stuart Kettlewell fired in a late, late winner as the Spiders hit back with a three goal salvo in the final ten minutes.

Gretna went in front three minutes after half time when Bingham dribbled his way into the box but was dispossessed by Reilly. The ball fell to Baldacchino who fired home from 15 yards. Five minutes later Bingham had a shot cleared off the line. The loss of David Holdsworth through injury appeared to unsettle Gretna's defensive stability and Queens pressed for an equaliser that arrived in the 80th minute when substitute Brian Felvus scored with a diving header.

Sixty seconds later Gretna regained the lead when Bingham headed in a Galloway free-kick.

Felvus then fired against the post and big Andy Smith was back to clear the danger. Frankie Carroll scrambled in the equaliser with six minutes to go after keeper David Mathieson appeared to be fouled under pressure. Queens grabbed the winner in the dying seconds when a right wing cross was only half cleared to Kettlewell who volleyed home. Angry boss Rowan Alexander said he was hurt and annoyed by the lack of commitment shown and that Gretna had got what they deserved from the game – nothing.

Gretna put things right with a 1-0 mid-week Bell's Cup second round win over Cowdenbeath at Raydale with Andy Smith on target and the Blue Brazil were back at Raydale on the Saturday for a league clash that saw two pieces of Samba magic from David Bingham win it 2-1.

Ryan Baldacchino had missed a penalty before Bingham's clever drag back and low centre set up Andy Smith to ram the opener into the roof of the net four minutes before the break.

And Bingham drilled the winner low into the bottom corner in the 62nd minute after a surging run from veteran centre half and assistant boss Davie Irons.

Cowden had levelled in the 54th minute when Dene Shields played in Paul McHale to beat the advancing Mathieson.

Bingham was causing concern as early as the fourth minute when he rose to head a pin-point Baldacchino cross inches over the bar from 12 yards.

And just three minutes later he latched onto a Danny Lennon cross and cleverly flicked over keeper Allan Fleming, but Innes Ritchie raced back to head off the line.

Smith was then just unable to stretch and get on the end of a Ryan McGuffie centre as Gretna kept up the pressure.

In the 29th minute Lennon played in Smith who was pulled down as he went around Fleming. Baldacchino, who along with Bingham was on the end of some heavy treatment from the Cowden players, stepped up to take the penalty and uncharacteristically blazed it over the bar.

But Gretna's dominance paid off when Smith hammered home following Bingham's brilliance in the box.

Cowden sub Stephen Bathgate got in behind the Gretna defence two minutes after the break, but Mathieson did well to parry away his powerfully struck volley.

Smith went down injured and was replaced by Kenny Deuchar and just a minute later McHale was sent through and poked his shot under Mathieson to level.

Gretna won it when Irons embarked on a run from the half way line and played into Bingham's feet just inside the area. Surrounded by three men, Bingham dropped his shoulder, feigned to go one way and sweetly smacked a left foot drive low into the net.

In the dying seconds Deuchar almost added a third as he lashed in a shot that Fleming blocked with his flailing arm at the near post and the big striker's follow up was diverted wide by a defender.

The club captured midfielder Bryan Gilfillan for £10,000 from Cowdenbeath during the week and he had cause for double celebration as he not had his twentieth birthday, but hit a last-gasp equaliser at promotion rivals Peterhead.

Gilfillan had been a target for both clubs, but decided to join the Raydale side. "Their keeper pulled off some great saves and I thought it wasn't going to be our day. I have to say sorry to Peterhead boss Iain Stewart. When I found out both clubs wanted to sign me, the fact Gretna are full-time swung it."

The versatile Gilfillan had played in a number of positions in his career and shrugged: "I still don't really know what my best position is. I've been a centre half then a right back and now up front. At Cowdenbeath I played everywhere across the back and it soon became everywhere across the middle and then I played up front."

Sub Gilfillan slid to poke a Mark Birch cross beyond keeper Paul Mathers in the last seconds after Peterhead had withstood a second half barrage after taking the lead in the 38th minute, Jamie Buchan playing a neat one-two with Martin Bavidge and curling the return into the top corner from the edge of the box.

Gretna crashed out of the Bell's Cup in a 3-0 quarter final defeat at the hands of classy First Division leaders Falkirk. The Bairns went in front with a freak goal in the 40th minute. Davie Irons hit a high backpass but keeper David Mathieson – sure it was a deflection – caught it cleanly. Referee Hugh Dallas awarded a direct free kick seven yards out and then cautioned the keeper for kicking the ball away. Trinidad and Tobago International Russell Latapy made Gretna pay the price, outfoxing the defensive wall to flash a shot into the net.

Andy Thomson made it 2-0 in the 63rd when he beat three defenders and drew Mathieson before sliding the ball into the empty net. Darryl Duffy rounded it off in the 73rd minute as he cut in from the right and powered in an unstoppable shot.

With Andy Smith sidelined due to a rib injury, Kenny Deuchar claimed the number nine shirt and hit a devastating second half hat-trick to demolish his old club East Fife 5-1 at Raydale. It was Deuchar's first full start of the season.

The Borderers went in front after only two minutes as

David Bingham beat his marker and fired a low shot into the net from 20 yards.

But East Fife equalised when keeper Mathieson brought down Leslie Byle and former Gretna player Brian Fairbairn fired home the penalty in the 26th minute.

The Fifers had a great chance to go in front when Fairbairn played the ball in to Kevin Steele, but he fired over the bar from eight yards.

Gretna had an ear bashing from manager Rowan Alexander at half time and it had the desired effect. They started with all guns blazing and were unlucky not to go ahead when Bryan Gilfillan thumped a shot against the post and Deuchar just missed firing home the rebound.

But Deuchar did put Gretna back in front when he towered above the visiting defence to head home Gavin Skelton's cross in the 51st minute.

David Irons and Skelton also went close but it was Fifers defender Craig Lumsden who made it 3-1 when he turned a Skelton cross past his own goalkeeper in the 62nd minute.

Six minutes later Deuchar grabbed Gretna's fourth from another testing Skelton corner and two minutes later he claimed his hat-trick, racing onto a through ball to fire home.

But Kenny didn't really want to celebrate his strikes out of respect for his old mates. "It's hard playing against an old club and East Fife's fans have always been really good to me and I had a great relationship with them," he admitted after the game.

"It was nice to score three, but I kind of wish it hadn't been against my old team. I felt it was not right to celebrate as I've a lot of respect for the club and their fans. But the Gretna fans applauded me too and I'm delighted they've taken to me," said Deuchar, who received an ovation from both sets of fans when he was substituted ten minutes from time.

"I must admit it has been frustrating watching from the sidelines until now. It's taken time to adapt to full-time football and I understand why I've been left out but I'm desperate to do well when given the chance," continued Deuchar, a fully qualified Doctor who hung up his stethoscope to go full-time at Raydale – save one day a week at Wishaw hospital to keep his hand in – during the summer.

Deuchar netted another as red hot winger Ryan Baldacchino provided the hammer blows with Gretna doing a demolition job on Elgin City with a 3-0 win at Raydale in the following fixture.

Baldacchino set up a David Bingham first half double and a towering Deuchar header as the Borderers ripped City apart.

In the 8th minute Baldacchino whipped in a free kick that was cleared only as far as Bryan Gilfillan who fired a stinging drive whistling just past the upright.

Baldacchino was tormenting City again soon after when he crossed from the right and Bingham's hooked volley fell wide.

Gretna went in front in the 21st minute when tough tackling midfielder Gilfillan swept play out to the right and Baldacchino whipped in a cross that Bingham stooped to head into the bottom corner.

Gavin Skelton then curled one over from the left and Deuchar climbed to send a looping header just wide.

City's Adam Nelson should have levelled when Harty played him in but keeper Davie Mathieson brilliantly saved his close range effort one-handed.

But Gretna had a great chance to double their lead in the 36th minute when the battling Gilfillan put Deuchar in and as the big striker went past keeper Keiron Renton, he was tripped and the ref pointed to the spot. Bingham stepped up but placed his low penalty wide of the post.

Bingham made amends just four minutes later when Baldacchino swung in a corner that Davie Irons flicked on and the goal ace was perfectly placed to fire home number two.

Two minutes before the interval Elgin's Ian Vigurs curled in a fantastic 25-yard free kick that had Mathieson at full stretch to parry away.

But Baldacchino was providing a constant menace and Gretna made it three in the 52nd minute when he beat Allan Dempsie and fired in a tempting centre that Deuchar sent rippling into the roof of the net with a thumping header.

Gretna could have added another when sub Brian Wake sent Bingham clear and as he squared into Ryan McGuffie's path, the tireless midfielder shot straight at Renton's legs.

Wake then cut in from the left and fired a powerful curling shot inches past the post and Deuchar flicked another header inches wide as the Borderers finished strongly.

Sub Stephen Cosgrove was denied in the last minute when his 20-yard thunderbolt looked destined for the top corner but Renton arched his back and spectacularly turned it over the bar. And the keeper again did brilliantly to block Irons' blasted close range volley from the resultant corner to keep the scoreline respectable.

While things were ticking along nicely up front, in the defence central defender Andy Aitken had been helping to avert disaster since singing from local rivals Queen of the South. And the six foot one inch Annan lad also ensured that the local community were prepared for any worst-case scenario as he worked part-time for Dumfries & Galloway Council's emergency planning department.

Twenty-six year old Aitken spent eight years at Palmerston Park, clocking up over 200 appearances and netting four goals as Queen's tasted success with promotion and a Bell's Cup trophy – giving Aitken a taste for silverware that he was keen to add to at Raydale after signing a three-year contract.

"Gretna really look after their players and all the boys are made to feel really special here. We have an excellent squad and anything less than promotion is out of the question," said Aitken.

"I dropped down two divisions to play for Gretna which was the only thing that went against moving here, but I spoke to Rowan Alexander and Brooks Mileson and the ambition they have for the club is phenomenal. Brooks has a five-year plan to get us into the Premier League and I want to be part of it."

Aitken had been a target of both Aberdeen and Carlisle United but opted to join Gretna.

The defence was again solid as they kept a clean sheet with Bingham and Deuchar again on target in a 3-0 win at Stenhousemuir.

Mark Birch had a 25-yard effort blocked before Gretna took the lead on 23 minutes when Deuchar powerfully headed home Bryan Gilfillan's cross from the right.

With Gretna dominating the game, Birch crossed from the right and Bingham dispatched a low shot past keeper McCulloch at the far post in the 57th minute. Bingham completed the scoring in the 83rd minute when he dispossessed

Tony Smith on the edge of the box and ran in to slip the ball past the advancing keeper.

Hot-shot Kenny Deuchar then plundered his second hat-trick of the season as Gretna's big guns pounded basement boys East Stirling like a Panzer Division.

Shell-shocked 'Shire were simply blown apart by the black and whites as the launched barrage after barrage in an 8-1 blitz at Raydale.

The game kicked off twenty minutes late after the visitor's coach was held up in heavy traffic on the motorway down. But if Gretna had any thoughts that the visitors had left their legs on the bus, they were shattered when 'Shire stunned Raydale into silence with the opener after just nine minutes.

Jamie Dunbar's right wing cross evaded the stretching Davie Irons and Derek Ure was left free to drill low past the exposed David Mathieson from 16 yards.

Gavin Skelton drove a low range effort just wide and Ryan Baldacchino blazed a volley over the angle as Gretna looked to hit back.

The leveller came in the 28th minute when a short free-kick was touched into the path of full-back Mark Birch who hammered an unstoppable 25-yard drive whistling into the bottom corner.

The game was turned on its head just two minutes later when Gretna broke the length of the pitch from a corner and Baldacchino clipped a cross to the far post for the unmarked Bryan Gilfillan to thump in a close range header.

Gilfillan turned provider in the 39th minute when he chipped into the box for Deuchar to head his first into the roof of the net.

'Shire were left reeling on the ropes again within two minutes when Deuchar's powerful header from a Baldacchino pin-point centre crashed in off the underside of the bar for number four.

After the break, Joe Robertson's spin and volley forced Mathieson into a superb diving save, but Gretna went straight back up the park and made it 5-1 with Gavin Skelton racing into the box and firing a low curling shot into the bottom corner with the outside of his boot from Bingham's pass.

And genius Bingham created number six in the 61st minute with an amazing back-heeled flick from a Birch cross for Deuchar to ram home at the second attempt.

Birch smashed in a piledriver that shaved the bar and Skelton forced keeper Ross Gilpin into a spectacular save as Gretna kept pouring forward.

They made it 7-1 in the 82nd with a great flowing move. Ryan McGuffie played in Stephen Cosgrove, and when Gilpin spilled his powerful shot, sub Brian Wake ruthlessly pounced to smash in from close range.

Winger Baldacchino completed the rout in stoppage time, controlling Bingham's chip on his chest and squeezing a low left foot shot just inside the post from nine yards.

Deuchar stood outside the dressing rooms in his club suit after the game, a slight frown on his brow, and groaned that referee Martin Sproule had tried to put one of his strikes down as an own goal.

But the prolific number nine, like all top poachers, was having none of it and insisted that his treble, his second in four games, was all his own.

"The ref tried to steal the second goal from me – but I'm keeping it!" he explained. "He said that the keeper's knocked it in but the ball came down off the bar and over the line from my header as far as I'm concerned." Just then gaffer Rowan Alexander appeared in the doorway with a grin and tossed Kenny the matchball, which he caught and cradled under his arm. The penny dropped – he'd been had by the dressing room pranksters.

"It doesn't matter how often the lads wind me up as long as I can keep firing in the goals," smiled Kenny. "That was my second hat-trick and I was delighted to keep on scoring. You're on a hiding to nothing against teams like East Stirling. Everyone expects you to win but they came here and took the lead and gave us a real fright. However we kept our cool and fought our way back into the game. Once the goals started to come we never looked back and those goals were real quality," said the 24-year-old six foot three inch forward.

The goals kept coming – though Deuchar didn't hit the net – in a 6-2 win at Albion Rovers. Gretna took the lead in the 31st minute when Baldacchino's left wing corner was only half cleared and David Bingham rose to head home.

Five minutes after the break it was 2-0 as Jamie McQuilken broke brilliantly down the left to beat keeper Mark Peat with a low shot. Mark Birch rifled the third into the top corner from 30 yards in the 58th minute. The fourth came in the 66th minute when Bingham robbed the keeper and cut the ball back to Deuchar who saw his shot blocked, but Skelton fired in the rebound.

With twenty minutes to go Deuchar set up Bingham who beat Peat with a delicate chip for number five.

Rovers sub John Bradford capitalised on slack defending to pull two back in the 73rd and 80th minutes, but Brian Wake slotted in the sixth two minutes later with the home defence appealing in vain for offside.

The goals kept raining in as Deuchar took his tally into double figures and Gretna exacted revenge for their defeat at Hampden by keeping their promotion charge at full throttle with a 4-1 over Queen's Park at Raydale.

Deuchar almost opened his account in just the fourth minute when Gavin Rushford's clearance looped off his shins and keeper David Crawford's heart was in his mouth as he had to catch it under the bar.

Deuchar had the crowd on their feet ten minutes later when he flicked the ball over the lunging Richard Sinclair and cracked a powerful 16 yard drive just the wrong side of the post and into the side netting.

Gretna went in front in the 23rd minute when Jamie McQuilken guided a chip into the box and Deuchar headed back for the inrushing Ryan McGuffie to control and fire a side-footed volley into the bottom corner of the net giving Crawford no chance.

Midfielder McGuffie silenced the doubters with that goal, his first of the season, and piled the agony on the bookies. The former Newcastle United youngster had been jokingly dubbed 'jigsaw' in the press by gaffer Rowan Alexander for 'going to pieces in the box.'

After seeing the ball ripple into the net, McGuffie had beamed: "It was written in the stars that I'd score. I've made a lot of people happy who had money on me to be first goalscorer. My dad Kenny had a tenner on me at 16-1 and some of the office staff got me at 9-1. My dad should definitely be weighing me in with a slice of his winnings!"

The hard-working central midfielder had been a consistently solid performer all season and had formed a formidable partnership with Bryan Gilfillan.

"I don't think the goal will be enough to get rid of the jigsaw tag because the gaffer's so chuffed that he's made up a name that's stuck," he groaned.

"It's just great to be off the mark because the goal has been a long time coming. The lads make more of me not scoring than I do because, as far as I'm concerned, the most important thing is that we win and it doesn't matter who scores."

Ryan put his university studies on hold and signed full-time during the summer – a move which he felt had benefited him on the park.

"Going from part-time to full-time football has helped make me a better player as I feel sharper, fitter and stronger and I'm pleased with the way things are going."

"Ryan certainly answered his critics with that goal," said boss Alexander.

"The lads had a little bet going on him scoring and if he keeps making runs the law of averages say he is going to score. He's a confident guy on and off the field and as long as he continues making his positive runs into the box the goals will come."

Five minutes after McGuffie struck, McQuilken split the Spiders defence with a brilliant through ball and Deuchar rounded the outrushing Crawford and fired a low shot past two defenders racing back before reeling away in celebration.

It was 3-0 in the 33rd minute. McQuilken launched a throw into the area, Deuchar flicked it on and Gavin Skelton span and volleyed in through a packed box.

Eight minutes later David Bingham swept play out to the right wing with a superbly effortless crossfield ball and when Ryan Baldacchino's centre was half cleared, Mark Birch thundered in a 25-yard drive that flashed just over the bar. And

Skelton stung Crawford's palms with another long range effort as Gretna finished the half strongly.

The Spiders came out battling after the break and Shaun Molloy was booked for an ugly sliding foul on McGuffie as Gretna had to tough it out and were allowed no time to settle on the ball.

Gretna's Bryan Gilfillan and Queen's Mark Ferry were next to have their names taken as the tackles flew in during a full-blooded encounter.

Queen's Park pulled one back in the 63rd minute when skipper Andy Aitken went to shepherd the ball out and was harshly adjudged to have tripped Frankie Carroll. Clark dispatched the spot-kick low to the right, sending Davie Mathieson the wrong way.

And the Spiders big hit-man Ally Graham was unlucky 15 minutes from time when he controlled on his chest and fired a volley just over from 16 yards.

But Gretna made it 4-1 with two minutes to play when sub Derek Townsley slid a perfect through ball to release Brian Wake and the former Carlisle hot-shot, his hair a mop of dark curls and sporting a goatee beard, didn't break stride as he raced in on goal and lashed across Crawford high into the net. It was the third successive game that the striker had come off the bench to score.

Gretna then thumped Cowdenbeath 8-0 at Central Park. When Mark Birch smashed in his first goal for Gretna on his debut against Stranraer the previous season, he admitted that he wasn't sure how to celebrate. But the popular right back was getting plenty of opportunities to practice punching the air after hitting a hat-trick, taking his tally to five in four games.

Dead-ball expert Birch thumped in a stunning eight-minute first half treble as Gretna kept up the pressure on leaders Peterhead with another emphatic victory.

Gretna took the lead in the 12th minute when Ryan Baldacchino cut the ball back to Ryan McGuffie who rifled into the net from 18 yards.

The lead was doubled on 20 minutes when a free-kick was touched to Birch who slammed a low shot into the bottom corner from 25 yards. Four minutes later Birch blasted in from the penalty spot after Kenny Deuchar had been brought down. He completed his hat-trick in the 28th minute with a carbon copy of his first goal.

Two minutes later Baldacchino shot home from close range and the first half scoring was completed on 36 minutes when David Bingham broke away to lob the ball over keeper Andy Carlin from the edge of the box. Gretna eased off after the break but went further ahead on 53 minutes when Deuchar knocked the ball down for Bingham whose shot took a slight deflection before beating Carlin.

Gretna resumed their domination and Deuchar saw his fierce shot touched onto the bar by the keeper.

Carlin did well again to deny Deuchar and Birch with splendid saves before the 'Doc' finally got on the scoresheet with three minutes remaining after David Bingham had set him up.

Bingham himself then headed a late winner in a 2-1 win over Peterhead and admitted: "We got lucky."

Just four minutes were left when Gavin Skelton curled over a corner, Andy Aitken flicked on and Bingham powered in a back-post header that sent a packed Raydale into raptures.

That crucial goal put the Black and Whites ahead of the Blue Toon in the title race for the first time.

But the former Dunfermline hero said afterwards: "We were pretty lucky, especially in the second half. However, we got a draw up at Peterhead which was the least we deserved and we'll take anything we can get. Maybe Peterhead will rue the chances that they missed, but that's football. I knew it was late when I scored but it's a good time to score a goal and then we just had to see the time out."

Boss Rowan Alexander agreed with his 15-goal striker and said: "We stole it at the end. We were under pressure for long spells but Bingham is great to have in the side because he produces the goals. Over the two games we've played with Peterhead I felt we deserved to win."

It was a great result for the Gretna manager, who was celebrating four years in charge at the club the following day, but his heart was in his mouth after ten minutes when a David Hagen corner was cleared only as far as Keith Gibson and when he lobbed it back in Robert Lynn's deflected shot was hooked off the line by veteran Davie Irons.

At the other end, winger Ryan Baldacchino let fly with an 18-yard volley that cannoned off keeper Paul Mathers' knees.

In the 16th minute Peterhead's Martin Bavidge played a great ball over the top and Kynn was denied by Mathieson. Within sixty seconds Gretna were in front.

Baldacchino went down the right and crossed to the far post where Gavin Skelton's powerful header was parried by Mathers and Bingham was on hand to fire into the roof of the net.

Gretna almost doubled their advantage in the 28th minute when Jamie McQuilken and Skelton combined down the left but McQuilken's pull back evaded the lurking Kenny Deuchar and was thumped clear.

Peterhead - unbeaten going into the game - hit back to level four minutes later.

Bavidge headed down Craig Campbell's deep cross for Lynn and he was bundled over by Aitken in the box. David Hagen stepped up and coolly netted the penalty.

But the Blue Toon escaped two minutes later when Mark Perry handled in the box but Gretna's penalty appeals were turned away by referee Mike Tumilty.

Two minutes after the break Skelton went close with a fierce half volley just wide and in the 53rd minute he played in Deuchar who crossed for Bingham but his first-time side-footed shot was blocked by Mathers.

Just before the hour Campbell played in Lynn who spun but his shot was saved by Mathieson at his near post.

Lynn, who had replaced top scorer Scott Michie in the starting eleven, went close again in the 69th minute when Jamie Buchan threaded a great ball through to him and he fired a low shot just inches wide. A minute later Campbell sent Lynn clear but Mathieson blocked his shot with his legs.

Peterhead looked dangerous on the break but had thir hearts broken four minutes from time when Bingham popped up for his second.

Blue Toon boss Iain Stewart said: "I can't complain about the way the boys played. I think the least we deserved was a draw and the boys are gutted. You can go on about chances but we came here and played a full-time team and you'd be hard pushed to say who the full-time team were. But football is not about chances, it's about goals and they got two and we got one."

Hit-man Kenny Deuchar then destroyed Albion Rovers at Raydale as he smashed in a stunning FIVE goals in a 6-2 win to stretch Gretna's lead at the top of the table. It took his tally to sixteen in just nine full starts for the club.

"That was unbelievable. I'm lost for words. Everything I touched in the second half went in – it was one of those days," he admitted afterwards.

Midfielder Bryan Gilfillan headed in a Mark Birch cross for the opener in the 17th minute and Deuchar made it two just three minutes later when he fired in from close range after a quickly-taken free-kick caught Rovers cold.

But the Cliftonhill side pulled one back just seconds before the break when Jed Stirling's long-range drive took a wicked deflection off skipper Andy Aitken and looped into the net.

Gretna came out guns blazing after the interval and Deuchar pounced to make it three a minute after the restart. He completed his hat-trick in the 53rd minute when Jamie McQuilken's fiercely hit shot cannoned down off the underside of the bar and he was on hand to net the rebound.

It was goal-King Kenny's third treble since his summer arrival at the ambitious Borders club.

Albion fought back and Paul McManus rounded David Mathieson to make it 4-2 in the 63rd minute.

But Deuchar displayed the Midas touch that had made him a firm terrace favourite at Raydale and netted number five eight minutes from time when he fired into the net from 15 yards after a great ball from strike partner David Bingham.

The tannoy was belting out 'Doctor, doctor give me the news,' for the fifth time three minutes before the end when Gavin Skelton set up the towering number nine to again stretch the net and reel away in celebration.

It was the third time that Gretna had hit Albion for six and Cliftonhill gaffer Kevin MacAllister praised the Raydale team.

"Their quality is there to be seen, they have got goals all over the place," said Crunchie. "I was at Falkirk with Kenny and I'm pleased for the big guy – although not so much today!"

Deuchar struck again in a 3-1 success at his old club East Fife as Gretna extended their lead at the top of the table to six points with a hard-fought victory at a rain-soaked Bayview.

Deuchar looped in a header from a Gavin Skelton cross to put Gretna one-up after 18 minutes. He then saw another header cleared off the line by Gary Kelly before Gretna went further ahead in the 35th minute when McDonald's slip let in Deuchar one-on-one with Morrison. The keeper blocked his effort but the ball broke to Baldacchino who slipped a shot into the net from 25 yards out.

East Fife were posing little threat but were handed a lifeline in first half stoppage time when Brian Fairbairn's right wing corner was cleared only as far as Stevie Nicholas, whose low shot sneaked in at the post.

The Fifers came out battling at the start of the second period but Gretna weathered the storm and as they regained authority, Gavin Skelton saw his 20-yard drive hit the side netting.

Baldacchino forced Morrison into a fine save before Gretna tied up the points with a decisive third goal. David Bingham put Brian Gilfillan through and he scored with a low shot after 84 minutes.

Grafter Gilfillan knew all about hard work – both on and off the pitch. When Inverness Caledonian Thistle released the tireless 20-year-old midfielder, he had to get a job on a building site in Edinburgh as well as fitting in training for part-timers Cowdenbeath.

Anyone who has shivered in the dust and wood shavings in a hard hat and steel toe capped boots on a site, lumping bags of cement about will let you know – construction is a tough game that teaches you to value what you've got. Forget Jimmy Nail, Dennis Healy and the boys in their donkey jackets with a bottle of Becks in one hand and a trowel in the other in Auf Weidersien, Pet. It's hard coin.

"I was up at six in the morning and grafting all day before going straight to training two nights a week. It wasn't fun," he admitted. But Gilfillan had the talent to get off the buildings and was delighted to be back in full-time football at Gretna – and it was an opportunity he was determined to make the most of.

"That's why I get annoyed when I see some boys at Gretna these days taking the game for granted. Believe me, that's a mistake. I feel like I've been given a second chance by Gretna, because I was at Caley as a kid and I didn't do myself justice. I'd rather have been lying in bed on my days off than battering myself down the gym. It wasn't good enough and when John Robertson took over he let me go." Gilfillan had made a huge impact since joining Gretna from the Blue Brazil with his surging runs, vision, passing and strong tackling all creating a massive headache for opponents.

Deuchar hit two more with David Bingham getting the other in a 3-1 win at Borough Briggs against Elgin before the former Highland Leaguers visited Raydale in the second round of the Tennent's SFA Cup. Winger Ryan Baldacchino had been a constant menace to City on the last league visit and he hoped to continue that form into the Cup tie.

"The season is going really well and being top of the league, we've got to keep it going," he said. "I've got five goals in the first half of the season and I'm hoping for at least another five in the second half. I'd like to get around fifteen and if the team keeps playing the way it has been, there's no reason why I shouldn't." Being top of the table and with a weight of expectation on the team to perform after the quality of players brought into the club didn't faze Ryan. "I think it's a pressure we thrive on really. Being under pressure to perform has brought the best out in the lads and we've gone 11 games undefeated. I had relegation pressure when I was at Carlisle but this is a different kind of pressure and the lads are excelling with it. It's a really good learning curve for me. The Third Division is hard and physical but I feel that can only benefit me. The physical aspect of the game in Scotland can only make me into a better player."

Baldacchino was again instrumental in the game as Kenny Deuchar struck twice in the 3-0 win to earn Gretna a third round tie at home to SPL Dundee United – and earned himself a run around in club owner Brooks Mileson's luxury Aston

Martin for a week. The towering striker left the field clutching a magnum of champagne after his man-of-the-match display and also had a bottle of whisky waiting for him in the dressing rooms after scooping the player of the month award for November as his fame was beginning to reach cult status throughout the country following Jeff Steling's rave reviews on the Sky Sports results service.

Brooks had promised his car for a week to any player hitting a hat-trick – and as Deuchar had played a major role in Gretna's other goal, which saw the unlucky Paul Kaczan put into his own net, the former East Fife ace was granted an unofficial treble.

In the tenth minute Baldacchino played a short corner to David Bingham who crossed for Ryan McGuffie to flash a powerful drive inches over from 10 yards.

Gretna had plenty of possession in the first half but the closest they came to breaking down a well-organised Elgin outfit was when Baldacchino's cross-shot flew over the helpless keeper Keiron Renton but thumped back off the bar.

But just 30 seconds after the break Baldacchino jinked in from the right wing and played in Bingham who rolled a clever pass to Deuchar to lash into the roof of the net.

The high-scoring Borderers got a lucky break ten minutes later when Deuchar got to the bye line and fired in a low centre that Kaczan steered past his own goalkeeper.

Deuchar added his 21st of the season three minutes later when he climbed to power in a header off the foot of the post from Baldacchino's deep free kick.

Gretna had further chances to increase their lead with Gavin Skelton shooting wide from a great position, sub Andy Smith just failing to connect with a brilliant Jamie McQuilken cross and Deuchar sending a blistering drive fizzing just inches past the post.

Stenhousemuir then made the trip down to the Border in the league. Gretna midfielder Stephen Cosgrove had a spell on-loan at the club the previous season as the Warriors battled relegation. The talented ball player enjoyed his time at Ochilview, but found it hard being involved in the Second Division drop-zone dogfight week-in, week-out.

"It was a good experience for me but it was probably the wrong time that I went because they were struggling. But it was great just being involved in first-team football and I think I learned a lot from it," said Cosgrove.

"I wasn't really happy with my performances. The team was struggling and low on confidence because it looked like they were going down. Getting beaten every week didn't do much for me but it was still a good experience to get first-team football."

Cosgrove went up to Stenhousemuir with veteran Raydale defender Keith Knox, who stayed up at the Maroons to become a lynchpin in their back line.

"I think Keith will have his work cut out. Deuchs and Bingy are flying just now and have hit 39 goals between them so it'll be hard for him, but he's also got plenty of experience so it'll also be a tough game for Kenny and David," he admitted.

Cosgrove had spent all season involved in the first team squad at Raydale and was keen to stake a claim in the starting eleven.

"I can just try and do my best. Obviously it's going to be hard to get into the first team just now as they're hammering teams every week so all I can really do is my best and hopefully get a chance."

Cosgrove spent the early part of his career training with some of the greatest names in the modern game at Old Trafford in the famous red shirt of Manchester United and was also in the SPL at Motherwell.

The likable Glasgow lad played alongside such huge stars as Ryan Giggs, David Beckham and Paul Scholes for one of the most successful managers ever – Sir Alex Ferguson.

While he admits he was gutted to be released by the Red Devils, Cosgrove could see that the level of competition for places at the club was immense.

"It was brilliant down there. The training, the facilities were first class and the players down there were brilliant as well. Sir Alex always spoke to me about back home and that, but he didn't really treat me any different to the other boys, you know, he was good with all the young boys."

"I was gutted when I was released but with the amount of players down there it was hard to get a game even in the reserve team. I saw the players they'd let go before me as well and there wasn't much chance. To make it there you've got to be really special."

Cosgrove felt it was an exciting time to be involved at Gretna and that the club was going places.

"Everything that you get down here, like the training and the facilities, being full-time, you just don't get that anywhere else in the Scottish Third, probably the Scottish Second as well, so it's brilliant to be part of. I've got to try and get my chance and when it comes along, just take it."

Gretna set a new winning record as they beat the Warriors 3-0 and Ryan McGuffie had a grin bigger than a kid opening presents on Christmas Day after smashing in a stunning goal.

The tireless midfielder chased down an attempted clearance, got to the bye line and cut in to fire a fierce shot across keeper Willie McCulloch and into the corner of the net from a narrow angle for Gretna's important second.

Boss Rowan Alexander described the strike as 'exceptional' and it was certainly worthy of breaking Inverness Caley Thistle's long-standing 11 straight wins Division Three record as well as taking Gretna a step nearer to a Championship medal as they went five points clear at the top of the table again.

McGuffie had earlier missed a great chance when he shot straight at McCulloch after Bingham's clever back-heel had set him up.

But you could be sure that when the 23-year-old got down to unwrapping on the 25th, a jigsaw set wouldn't be among the boxes under his tree.

Gretna got off to a great start and were celebrating the opener after their first attack in the fourth minute. Gavin Skelton won a tremendous tackle to play in Kenny Deuchar and the bustling striker broke through and squared for the in-sliding Bingham to fire into the bottom corner.

Stenhousemuir were unlucky not to level ten minutes later when dangerman Joe Savage saw his 20-yard drive cannon back off the angle of bar and post. The Warriors were moving the ball around the pitch confidently and Savage was again denied by a brave block by Davie Irons before McGuffie drilled in his wonder strike to make it 2-0 in the 36th minute.

Then Skelton shot wide at the near post and Ryan Baldacchino went through but McCulloch stood up well and saved his shot.

David Bingham was full of tricks and he produced another back heel to put Baldacchino in, but the tricky winger rushed his shot and blazed over the bar in the 54th minute.

Stenhousemuir felt aggrieved twelve minutes later when veteran Keith Knox went down in the box under a challenge from Irons but referee Brian Winter waved away their strong penalty appeals.

And Gretna made it three in the 73rd minute when Jamie McQuilken curled in a tempting centre for Bryan Gilfillan to glance a header past the helpless McCulloch.

Top scorer Kenny Deuchar will still be scratching his head as to how he didn't add to his tally after having a hat-trick of goals flagged for offside during the game.

Stenny's misery was compounded in the last minute when Robbie Henderson was sent off for a second yellow after chopping Deuchar down.

Gretna then ground out a 3-2 New Year's Day win at Montrose's Links Park in difficult conditions.

Montrose went in front in the 17th minute when Martin Wood's pass split the Gretna defence and Graeme Sharp ran on to slip the ball past Davie Mathieson. But Gretna were level within 90 seconds as Gavin Skelton's shot looped off a defender's foot and into the path of Kenny Deuchar who headed past Jim Butter. Montrose looked unsettled and it was no surprise when Deuchar headed in a Baldacchino cross for his second in the 24th minute.

With the atrocious conditions causing problems for both defences, Montrose drew level again seven minutes later when Euan Hall volleyed in from 15 yards as a corner was only half cleared.

Almost from the kick-off Gretna hit the winner when Baldacchino's angled drive appeared to take a deflection past Butter.

David Bingham was then the goalscorer in a 1-1 draw at Hampden Park with Queen's Park as the winning run was halted before Gretna's eagerly awaited Tennent's SFA Third Round tie against Dundee United fell victim to the weather twice.

David Holdsworth had been out injured since the August defeat at Hampden and he hung up his boots before his persistent back problems meant he was unable to pick up his baby son, Charlie. The vastly-experienced defender had decided to call a day on his playing career but continued at the club as a youth and diet and fitness coach.

"I'm not walking away, but I am bright enough to know it's the right decision to make at this time. I want to finish playing while I'm still fit and healthy and move my career into a new era. I'm thoroughly enjoying my time at Gretna and my wife and I are very settled in Cumbria. I'm content I've played a part in the new structure of the club and I love being part of the coaching set up," he said.

Classy new signing Davie Nicholls went straight into the team as Gretna kept up their march for the title with a 2-0 home win over Cowdenbeath. Midfielder Nicholls was signed from Falkirk on the Friday on a two-and-a-half year deal. The 32-year-old had returned to Brockville from Dunfermline in 2003 following a loan deal and had also played at Clydebank, Hibs, Cork City and Ayr United.

He replaced the injured Ryan Baldacchino for his debut as Gretna created a huge number of chances.

Kenny Deuchar put them ahead in the second minute but had a day of near misses. He blasted past the post, over the bar and against the upright as he tried desperately to find the net for a second time.

His opener came when David Bingham crossed and he gave keeper Andy Carling no chance with a powerful right foot shot.

Gretna hit the second in the 25th minute when Bingham slipped the ball out to Gavin Skelton and the number eleven hit a tremendous low shot into the net.

In the 65th minute Deuchar was left clear in front of goal. He looked to have calmly stroked the ball into the empty net but somehow it hit the upright and came out.

Jamie McQuilken had been eagerly anticipating lining up against his old club Dundee United in the Tennent's Cup on the Monday night and felt that Gretna had a great chance of causing an upset due to their exceptional form at Raydale Park.

The classy full-back made a £150,000 move from Celtic to Tannadice Park earlier in his career and made 24 appearances between 1995-97 at United.

"When the draw was made there was a big cheer from the dressing room so it's a game that the full squad is looking forward to, and we feel we have a reasonable chance of taking something from the game – especially with the home form we've shown this season, so the whole place has been looking forward to it," said McQuilken.

"You always want a big name in the Cup, especially at home, we've got a nice Premier side at home and you can't ask for any more than that. It'll give us an indication of how far we've come as a team and how far we've still got to go as a team."

McQuilken feared he may have to sit out the Second Round game against Elgin as he was on-loan from St. Johnstone and boss John Connolly didn't want him Cup-tied – but was delighted to make his move to Raydale permanent by signing a two-and-a-half year deal on the eve of the fixture.

"I was over the moon to sign," said McQuilken. "I played in a reserve game on the Thursday before the last round tie, obviously thinking that I wouldn't be playing on the Saturday, but the manager phoned me that night after the game and said an arrangement had been made with St. Johnstone so I should be free to play on the Saturday – I was delighted."

Thirty-year-old McQuilken earned himself a week in Managing Director Brooks Mileson's Jaguar after a man of the match performance against Stenhousemuir – including setting up the third goal for Bryan Gilfillan – and had proved a key member of the squad.

"The team has been playing really well. The home form is exceptional. We've been winning games convincingly both home and away and have been going really well but nothing has been achieved yet although we've given ourselves a big chance to get where we want to go. As long as we're in that position at the end of the season, everyone will be delighted."

McQuilken had played at the highest level but the cup had lost none of it's magic for him. "I've played for and against Dundee United so it's an interesting tie. I actually fancied United at Tannadice before the draw was made, so to get them at home is a bonus. It should be a really good game."

"None of my old-team-mates are left at United – it's a totally changed squad and obviously the management's changed as well, but knowing Ian McCall he'll have them well fired up and well organised for the game."

A temporary stand was erected at the South End of the ground and 3,000 excited people packed into Raydale, courtesy of Brooks Mileson who bought up the tickets for both the Gretna and United fans in a tremendous gesture to thank the loyal fans for their support. He also made a hefty donation to the United Supporters' trust.

Midfield enforcer Richard Prokas sparked the Gretna fight back as United were given a huge scare under the floodlights in a Scottish Cup thriller that had it all.

The tough tackling former Carlisle ace's ball-winning, work-rate and distribution were first class as the Borderers stormed back from 3-0 down to set up a nail-biting finale.

When winger Ryan Baldacchino hobbled off after taking a couple of heavy knocks to his recently injured ankle, Prokas came off the bench to add some steel to the Gretna engine room.

And he had been on the pitch just six minutes when he chased down a ball into the corner. There looked little danger with two defenders on top of him, but he squeezed a low centre to Bryan Gilfillan whose powerful shot was parried by keeper Tony Bullock and Kenny Deuchar pounced to fire the rebound low into the net.

Prokas said: "I felt we showed them a bit too much respect in the first half, but when David Mathieson saved the penalty and we got a goal back it gave us a lifeline. We got at them in the second half and created a few chances that on another day could have gone in. We gave a good account of ourselves."

Gretna found themselves a goal down after just three minutes when James Grady crossed from the right and Barry Robson climbed to thump a header into the net.

Just four minutes later United broke at pace with a slick passing move and when the ball broke free, Mark Kerr blasted a 25-yard drive into the top corner to make it two.

Hit-man Deuchar got his first sight of goal two minutes later when David Bingham back heeled into his path and he smashed in a 20-yard volley that stung Bullock's palms.

Mark Birch then had the bumper crowd on their feet with a thumping shot that flashed just over the angle.

But the SPL side went three up with a controversial penalty after only 19 minutes. Jamie McQuilken was harshly adjudged to have handled and after being mobbed by the Gretna players, referee Charlie Richmond went to consult his linesman - and to Gretna's disbelief he stuck to his guns and pointed to the spot. Mark Wilson drilled home the resultant kick sending Mathieson the wrong way.

And it could have been worse for Gretna in the 37th minute when the out-rushing Mathieson brought down Robson as he bore down on goal. Wilson smashed his second penalty the same way but Mathieson saved brilliantly and Grady blasted the rebound over the bar.

That proved a turning point and Bingham shaped to hit a fine volley inches wide before Deuchar struck to make it 3-1 five minutes before the break.

The never-say-die Third Division leaders needed just a minute of the second period to get another back - but in bizarre circumstances.

Ryan McGuffie fired in a high cross from the right and as Deuchar was pulled down, Gavin Skelton smashed into the roof of the net from close range. The Gretna players had already celebrated and placed the ball back on the centre spot when ref Richmond marched up and took the ball back down the field for a penalty for the foul on Deuchar. He waved away their protestations but Birch kept his cool to step up and crack in the spot kick.

Tangerines boss Iain McCall watched on nervously as the skilful Bingham ghosted past three challenges and set up

Gilfillan whose vicious drive was turned over the bar by Bullock.

Scotland striker Stevie Crawford eased the pressure as he raced onto a ball over the top to lift a wonderfully controlled lob over the stranded Mathieson for the crucial fourth.

But on two other occasions Crawford looked clean through on goal, only for Davie Irons, the oldest player in the Scottish League at 43, to produce breathtaking last-ditch tackles to deny the Terrors' man.

Gretna hit back when Bingham was chopped down 30-yards from goal and Skelton was teed-up to smash an unstoppable strike rocketing into the top corner beating Bullock at full stretch.

Prokas was relishing the challenge and driving Gretna on with great gusto but with the clock ticking down Deuchar was twice denied by Bullock and United hung on for a fourth round meeting with Queen of the South at Palmerston.

Their white shirts stained brown with mud, hair plastered to their foreheads with sweat and lashing rain, the Gretna players applauded the crowd as they trooped off the pitch with their heads held high.

Boss Rowan Alexander said: "I thought at 3-2 we had the game by the scruff of the neck but we suffered a sucker punch when they went up the park and scored the fourth. At 3-0 we had a lot of belief in the side and we have a group of high quality players who can take the club forward. The sky's the limit really and we have the ambition and the resources."

Gretna had tasted the top-flight and again displayed their ambitions with the audacious signing of top-class Aberdeen midfielder Stevie Tosh, who was given a baptism of fire on his black and white debut as they went down 4-2 at title rivals Peterhead in a top-of-the-table clash at Peterhead that put the Blue Toon within two points of Gretna with a game in hand.

Tosh signed from the Premier League Dons on the eve of the fixture and went straight into the team. The talented 31-year-old midfielder put pen to paper on a three-and-a-half-year contract and revealed that the Raydale challenge would be the biggest test of his career. His previous clubs included Arbroath, St. Johnstone, Raith Rovers, Livingston and Falkirk. He made his Aberdeen debut against Wolfsburg in 2003 and played 70 games for the Reds, netting nine times.

"This is a new start for me, although it will be a hell of a leap for me to go from playing the Old Firm to playing in the Third Division," he said.

"But I will be playing with quality players and Gretna have invested a lot of faith in me by giving me a lengthy contract. I have faced a few challenges in my time, but this is the biggest one."

The ex-Pittordrie ace put the long-term financial security of his family first, and was looking forward to linking up with his new team-mates on the pitch.

"I am leaving the third biggest club in the country – any other clubs outside the Old Firm who think they are bigger than Aberdeen are kidding themselves – and I thoroughly enjoyed my time at Aberdeen, even last season when things were not going well."

"But these things happen, you just have to get on with it. I wanted to secure my future and although leaving Aberdeen is disappointing, it is a great chance for me at Gretna."

It was a subdued Gretna party who jetted out for a sunshine break at a Spanish winter training camp in La Manga on the Monday morning as they went down 4-2 at Peterhead and the title race was narrowed to just two points, with the Blue Toon also having a game in hand.

It was goal-less at the break but just a minute into the second period Bryan Gilfillan powered into the Peterhead box and was bundled over by Robbie Raeside. Mark Birch smashed in the opener from the spot.

Martin Bavidge's pace and shooting power turned the game on it's head however in the 62nd minute. He chested down a Jamie Buchan cross and fired a shot past Mathieson and in off the post.

Seven minutes later he sliced open the Gretna defence, got to the bye-line and cut the ball back for Graeme Stewart to turn and beat Mathieson from two yards.

In the 72nd minute Bavidge won a corner on the left. Jamie Buchan flighted it in and defender Craig Tully rose to bullet a header into the top corner of the net for 3-1.

Gretna's misery was compounded ten minutes later when a Bavidge shot was deflected and as Davie Irons and Jamie McQuilken struggled to clear, Scott Michie nipped in to tap the ball home.

Ryan McGuffie added a second for Gretna in the last minute.

His midfield partner Gilfillan's red-hot form was rewarded with an International call-up from Northern Ireland. The hard-working 20-year-olds impressive performances had raised eyebrows at the IFA and Gilfillan was included in the U21 squad to face Scotland at Lansdowne Road.

BBC pundit and former Scotland boss Craig Brown had heaped praise on Gilfillan for his top-class display against Dundee United and IFA coach Roy Miller contacted the club after talking to Gilfillan's grandparents.

Gretna coach Danny Lennon was a former Northern Ireland full International star and he reckoned being capped by the Province would be an amazing experience for the tough-tacking youngster.

"It's absolutely fantastic and will give the boy a real confidence boost," said Lennon.

"He's been great since he came to the club from Cowdenbeath and it's brilliant for both Bryan and the club. It's good the Northern Irish FA are looking as far afield as the Scottish Third Division and it shows the direction the club is going," continued the ex-Partick Thistle captain.

"It's always good to go and mix with quality players and for Bryan to go and rub shoulders with the top players in the Northern Ireland squad would be great for him."

"I always found when I went away on International duty that I always came back with a lot of confidence. I don't think Bryan will be fazed as for a young player he has a mature mind and for him to come to Gretna and hold his midfield position speaks volumes for him," said Lennon, who also qualified to play for Northern Ireland through his grandparents.

George Best is probably the greatest player to pull on the famous green shirt and he made 37 appearances for Northern Ireland, scoring nine goals - and he controversially had one chalked off when he netted after cheekily nicking the ball off England keeper Gordon Banks' toes as he went to clear up field.

Gretna managing director Brooks Mileson took the news of Northern Ireland's interest out to Gilfillan and boss Rowan Alexander at La Manga when he jetted out to join the team. And in typically generous style, Brooks took the entire staff across to Ulster to watch Gilfillan's debut.

Poor East Fife must have feared the worst as Gretna made three more signings before the January window closed.

Hit-man David Graham reckoned the switch to full-time football would make him an even bigger menace to defenders. The club record £50,000 signing from Stranraer had attracted interest from Sheffield Wednesday and Aberdeen before being snapped up by Gretna.

"Full-time football will get me fitter and sharper and that's why I have come here," said Graham, who combined working as a clothes shop assistant with playing for the Blues.

"I am delighted with the chance and I'm looking forward to the challenge. Gretna aren't going to be a Division Three club for long and they have SPL ambitions like myself. I want to play at the highest level I can and hopefully that will be with Gretna. We have the best players outside the SPL and I'm really happy with the move because I believe we can win things."

Experienced Morton full-back Derek Collins joined from Cappielow and exciting young striker Dene Shields was also signed. Defender Chris Innes put pen to paper from Premier League Dundee United the day before the game.

But it was former East Fife man Kenny Deuchar who haunted his former team-mates with a hat-trick for the second time in a 4-0 win at Raydale.

Debutant Innes added the other, but it was a case of the ecstasy and the agony for the big centre back as he was stretchered off and taken to hospital with a nasty gash to his shin just five minutes after he celebrated hitting the net.

It was a sad sight as an ambulance was backed up to the dressing rooms to take Innes to the Cumberland Infirmary. "It's a bad one," said Rowan Alexander. "Chris has a gash of four to five inches just inside his shin guard so we're taking him to hospital to get him stitched up and he should be alright. He's done well, especially to get a goal on his debut - but we just can't get Davie Irons retired."

Deuchar picked up the keys to both Brooks Mileson's Aston Martin and Jaguar after being named man of the match and his goal exploits - but his opener owed much to a player who was like a Lamborghini on the pitch, David Bingham.

After just two minutes Bingham tied defender Kevin Bain in knots on the edge of the box by twice deftly flicking the ball up then sublimely lifting it over his shoulder into the path of Deuchar who blazed a low volley into the corner of the net.

Seven minutes later Jamie McQuilken picked out Deuchar with a flighted pass over the top and the Gretna goal-machine clipped the ball past on rushing keeper Scott Morrison before calmly knocking number two into the empty net.

Skipper Andy Aitken took a leaf out of Bingham's book when he hooked over his shoulder to set up Gavin Skelton, but Morrison brilliantly turned the midfielder's curling shot around the post.

Bingham then went close when his excellent first touch from Skelton's long ball took him past Michael Renwick but he fired over the bar from a narrow angle.

Gretna were dominating the proceedings and Morrison had to beat out quick to save at the feet of Gilfillan before East Fife were reduced to ten men on the stroke of half time when Gary Kelly saw red for a second booking.

As the tempo of the game dwindled, Gretna sent on record signing David Graham in the 54th minute and with his first touch in a black and white shirt he had the crowd on their feet as his thunderous drive from 20-yards crashed back off the crossbar.

On the hour Bingham's shot was parried at full stretch by Morrison and Graham lifted the rebound to the far post for Deuchar to power in a header, but Morrison recovered and scrambled across goal to beat away.

Bingham's trickery in the box created another chance for Graham that was blocked on the line by Kevin Steele and crambled to safety.

In the 79th minute Graham fired in a volley from the edge of box that Morrison turned over and from Skelton's resultant er, Innes headed in number three.

But Innes then thumped into a tough fifty-fifty challenge with former Raydale striker Brian Fairbairn that saw both players taken off the pitch.

Deuchar added the fourth with five minutes to play when he guided a looping header over Morrison's despairing outstretched hand from a pin-point Stevie Tosh cross.

After such an impressive display it was a bit of a surprise when it took a last-gasp winner from Derek Townsley to beat Elgin 2-1 in the next fixture at Raydale Park.

The hairs stood up on the back of Townsley's neck as his late goal sparked electric celebrations on the terraces that crackled in his head like static and sent the Borderers six points clear at the top of the table.

Townsley's winner deep into injury time also spared the blushes of midfielder Steve Tosh who could only look on in horror when City keeper Keiron Renton had earlier saved his penalty.

The seconds were ticking down and it seemed like Gretna's chance had gone when Hugh Dickson frantically cleared Gavin Skelton's header off the line. But sub David Graham whipped the ball back in from the right and Ryan McGuffie headed on for Townsley to pounce and fire into the net side-footed from close range.

With Gretna getting as desperate as a bachelor at kicking-out time, the ground erupted and Townsley was mobbed by his delighted team-mates.

"You could feel the tension in the place," admitted Townsley. "Elgin sat in and were very difficult to break down but we got the rub of the green in the end. It's only my second start since August, so looking back over the game I was quite pleased with my performance. You could sense the relief when the shot went in and it was pleasing to see it hit the back of the net."

Elgin took a shock lead in the 32nd minute when Andy Roddie stepped up and bent a superb 25-yard free kick over the wall and crashing into the net past keeper David Mathieson's full-stretch dive.

But Gretna took only two minutes to hit back as Kenny Deuchar powered in a header from a Skelton corner that the sprawling Renton parried and David Bingham popped up in the ensuing goalmouth scramble to poke in from four yards.

Gretna had a great chance to go in front in the 59th minute when they were awarded a penalty as Tosh flighted in a cross to the far post and Townsley's downward header struck Dickson's hand.

With regular taker Mark Birch out injured and replaced by experienced debutant Derek Collins, the former Aberdeen ace took responsibility and went for placement over power from the spot but cringed as Renton dived to save low to his left before Tosh was surrounded by goading City players.

"Big Degs has dug us out of a hole and I think I'm due to buy him a few pints for sparing my blushes," said Tosh after the game. "That's me finished with taking penalties. In future there's another ten guys in the queue ahead of me who will take them - including the goalie!"

Gretna brought David Graham and Dene Shields off the bench in an effort to break down the hard-working Highlanders and after McGuffie had fired a volley wide, Shields cut in from the left and let fly with a fierce shot which was deflected and Renton adjusted his body brilliantly to save.

Never-say-die Townsley's late winner maintained Gretna's 100% home record but was a real kick in the teeth for City and their frustration showed when Willie Martin was sent off for an ugly foul just seconds before the final whistle.

Then a second half hat-trick by Kenny Deuchar saw Gretna extend their lead at the top of the table with a 4-1 success at Stenhousemuir.

In strength-sapping conditions at Ochilview, the hosts set about Gretna and took the lead after three minutes when Paul McGrillen's in swinging corner from the right appeared to elude everyone and skidded into the net.

Gretna's response was immediate and Deuchar and David Bingham had efforts blocked before Derek Townsley prodded in the equaliser in the 13th minute when the home defence failed deal with a Mark Birch free kick.

Chances were squandered at both ends with Gretna having biggest let off as Joe Savage's effort was cleared off the line dying minutes of the first half.

Gretna assumed total control after the break and it was no surprise when they went in front in the 62nd minute as Townsley controlled Steve Tosh's free kick and cut the ball back for Deuchar to fire home.

He struck twice more in the 79th and 80th minutes. Firstly he delicately headed in a Gavin Skelton cross and sixty seconds later fired home from close range after keeper McCulloch had blocked his initial effort.

Boss Rowan Alexander reckoned the Borderers needed to get crocked right winger Ryan Baldacchino back into action to re-find top gear after a 4-1 win over Montrose at Raydale left the club just one win from promotion in record-breaking time.

The skilful wide-man had been out with a foot injury since the New Year, but the Gretna gaffer hoped to have him fit for the visit to East Stirling, where three points would see the club up into Division Two.

"It's been very noticeable that we've missed Ryan," said Alexander. "It was very poor all-round. The player to take praise from the game was David Bingham - without him I don't think we would have created anything. Our defending was atrocious for the second week running."

Bingham had a hand in three of the black and white's goals the saw them shatter the Third Division's previous goalscoring record of 87 held by Stranraer and Ross County.

Montrose striker Martin Wood raced through and rounded keeper David Mathieson to slot in the opener on 27 minutes.

But the leaders levelled right on half time when Bingham played in Gavin Skelton to fire in off Jim Butter's body.

Skelton bent in a corner for hit-man Kenny Deuchar to power in a near post header in the 56th minute and Mark Birch smashed in a spot-kick three minutes later after Kerr Dodds had been dismissed for halting Bryan Gilfillan's powerful run with a foul in the box.

Deuchar added his 30th league goal of the season when he drilled in Bingham's clever flick from 16 yards on 75 minutes.

Sub David Graham saw his lob from ten yards just clear the bar and Derek Townsley was unlucky not to add a fifth in the final minute when his looping header thumped back off the foot of the post.

"We need to identify the weakness in the defence but fortunately I have Chris Innes available for selection next week as well," said Alexander.

After a trip to basement boys East Stirling was postponed due to the weather, it was with a 1-0 victory at Central Park, Cowdenbeath that Gretna secured promotion - with two months of the season still to play.

Delighted Stevie Tosh fired the club into Division Two with a spectacular overhead kick and beamed: "It was great to score the goal that took us up - but now we want the title."

The former Aberdeen man hit the winner from a Kenny Deuchar cross after thirty minutes, acrobatically smashing into the roof of the net of the post to cap a fine man-of-the-match performance.

Tosh's winner sparked a Champagne celebration in the dressing rooms afterwards as MD Brooks Mileson's magnum - which he had kept on ice for a fortnight - showered the players and boss Rowan Alexander.

Gretna started well and Deuchar had a shot deflected for a corner after strike partner David Bingham had set him up.

Cowdenbeath were dangerous on the break and Gary Fusco shot just wide in the 23rd minute.

Deuchar fired against the woodwork before Tosh grabbed the goal that sent Gretna up in the Borderers next attack.

Cowden battled back and Darren Gribben forced Davie Mathieson into a fine save to keep his clean sheet intact.

Jamie McQuilken had a shot blocked but Cowden then enjoyed a good spell of pressure with Mathieson saving well from McCallum and Gribben in quick succession.

Having weathered the storm Gretna retained their composure and Ryan Baldacchino and sub Dene Shields came close. Gretna finished well on top with Tosh stinging the hands of Cowden keeper Andy Carling with a 20-yard free kick in the dying minutes as the travelling support began their celebrations.

The success was tinged with sadness as former Chairman Ian Dalgliesh passed away on the day of the fixture. Big Ian was a man with fire in his belly. Passionate about his 'good lass' Vi, Gretna FC, boxing, the British Army, animals, craftsmanship. He loved a joke and could tell you where to get the best fish and chips - and pint - in towns all across Scotland and the North of England.

He talked proudly about the clubs FA Cup exploits and how Gretna, then in the Northern League, could take on and beat Conference clubs 'for funsies.' How they should have beaten Bolton in the Cup, how they did beat Glasgow Rangers in a Lockerbie Disaster Charity match - 'And they didn't like it.'

Big Ian Dalgliesh was a football man. He saw Egypt and the Suez Canal in the army and worked for years at 'the pond' for BNFL at Chapelcross but foremost he loved to talk football.

Riding his bike down to the ground with a bag of sweets in his pocket for any person or animal he met on the way, Ian was a kind, warm-hearted man with a heart as big as his personality.

"I'm away to see the good lass and put an egg in the pan," he'd say as he left Raydale where he'd been involved since the club was formed in 1946.

He'd cut the grass, do up the stands, build terracing, was secretary, vice-chairman, chairman and life member and his brother-in-law designed the club crest; he'd been there from the very start.

"Ian was a great ambassador for Gretna FC and he put a lot of work into building the club from nothing," said manager Rowan Alexander.

"His brash approach to the job was historic and he built up tremendous ties with the North East clubs and people. His knowledge of players and clubs was staggering and he always had a story to tell. Never renowned for his shyness, he always made time to speak to you and made sure you spoke to him, because if you didn't, before you put a foot by him, his wrath swept by you like hurricane. Ian will be sorely missed in and around the club."

Ian would have been proud as the club followed up the promotion success with a 4-0 win at East Stirlingshire.

The black and whites raced into an early two goal lead, the first coming from a neat move between David Bingham and Ryan McGuffie, the hard-working midfielder setting up the tricky striker to finish coolly in the ninth minute.

Gretna hit their second just two minutes later with Bingham again at the heart of things.

Marauding full-back Jamie McQuilken began the move with a run out of defence and, after exchanging passes with Bingham on the edge of the area, slotted a low drive past 'Shire's Derek Jackson.

Bingham almost made it three during this spell of one-way traffic towards the 'Shire goal, but Jackson pulled off a flying save to divert his header for a corner.

Bingham was a class act for Gretna as he continued to provide openings for his mates and his pass to Kenny Deuchar should have led to the number nine getting on the scoresheet. However, he drove straight at Jackson but fortunately for Gretna, sub Davie Nicholls was on hand to lash in the rebound.

Gavin Skelton provided the cross for Ryan Baldacchino to net Gretna's fourth but the celebrations were marred by an injury to Bingham who had to be led from the field.

Gretna's misfortune continued when defender Andy Aitken was red-carded for a collision with 'Shire's Ross Donaldson and the referee sent him packing as he was the last line of defence.

Gretna hit four more at home to Queen's Park and Spiders full-back will still be having nightmares as he was given a torrid time by tricky winger Ryan Baldacchino.

David Bingham and Gavin Skelton were also in sparkling form as already-promoted Gretna produced a Champagne display that put them ten points clear at the top.

Gretna gave an early warning shot when Bingham cut the defence apart with a cleverly weighted ball that Baldacchino raced onto and Jon Whelan was forced to turn his dangerous near post ball behind for a corner.

Then Skelton whipped in a centre and Kenny Deuchar didn't break stride as he fired a fierce 16-yard drive inches wide with keeper David Crawford rooted to the spot.

The demolition job began in the 13th minute when the deadly trio combined for the opener.

Bingham lifted the ball over the top and the flying Baldacchino crossed for Skelton to guide a lob into the net from 8 yards.

And in the 24th minute Derek Collins touched a quick free kick to the skilful Baldacchino who fired in a centre for

Bingham to climb highest and power in a brilliant header off the underside of the bar.

Two minutes later Chris Innes pumped a long ball into the path of Deuchar who crossed for Bingham to stretch and hook his shot into the top corner of the net for 3-0.

Baldacchino jinked through and Trouten was lucky to escape with a yellow card as he chopped down the winger when he looked clean through on goal.

Just before half time Baldacchino curled over a cross and Skelton touched back for Bingham to sting Crawford's palms with a volley from the edge of the box.

Queen's boss Billy Stark spared Trouten further torture when he was subbed at the break – but Gretna took just twenty seconds to add number four.

Bingham flicked on Baldacchino's cross and Skelton held off Stuart Kettlewell before cracking low into the net.

Skelton was denied a brilliant hat-trick – and Gretna's 100th League goal of the season – when Baldacchino swept into his path and he slid a low shot under the advancing Crawford, but sub Gavin Rushford raced back to clear off the line.

Gretna took their foot off the gas but sub David Graham almost added number five late on as he outpaced the defence and fired in a volley that Crawford turned round the upright at full-stretch.

Off the park, Gretna appointed highly experienced coach Viv Busby Director of the Youth Academy.

Viv had a glittering playing career at Luton, Newcastle, Fulham, Norwich, Stoke, Sheffield United and Blackburn and had a spell in the USA with Tulsa.

Since hanging up his boots he was Denis Smith's number two at York City and Sunderland before taking up the managers role at Hartlepool. He moved to Sheffield United and was then Howard Kendall's assistant at Everton before coaching in Greece with Ethnikos then reserve coach at Fulham and youth boss at Swindon Town.

Kenny Deuchar grabbed his sixth hat-trick of the season and a place in the record books as Gretna laid one hand on the title trophy with a 6-1 mauling of closest rivals Peterhead at Raydale.

Deuchar's treble equalled the great Jimmy Greaves' record haul for a single campaign as the Raydale men demolished the Blue Toon.

Goal King Kenny netted Gretna's 100th league goal after just three minutes when Ryan Baldacchino sent over a pin-point cross and the towering hit-man powered a header into the roof of the net from 6 yards.

The Borderers were in the driving seat and were denied a second when Gavin Skelton curled over a corner and Mark Perry cleared Chris Innes' header off the line in the 27th minute.

Peterhead battled to get back into the game after the break but were restricted to thumping long hopeful balls forward with Keith Gibson flashing a volley wide and David Hagen having penalty appeals waved away after being clipped by Derek Collins.

Baldacchino was in fantastic form, crossing from the right again in the 61st minute and when David Bingham's clever flick hit Robbie Raeside, the rebound fell to Ryan McGuffie who thumped in an absolute screamer from 25-yards.

The game was effectively killed just sixty seconds later when Deuchar knocked down Baldacchino's cross and Bingham flashed in a low rising drive that Mathers got a hand too but it crashed up into the top corner of the net.

The Blue Toon pulled one back in the 70th minute when Hagen's in swinging corner was adjudged to have hit Deuchar's hand and Bavidge tucked away coolly from the penalty spot.

Gretna made it 4-1 in the 77th minute when Deuchar charged down a free kick in his own half and Skelton's crossfield ball sent Baldacchino away down the right to cross for McGuffie to power in a header.

Three minutes from time Deuchar pounced to lash in another Baldacchino cross and in the dying seconds 'the Doc' completed his sensational hat-trick as he raced onto a David Graham flick and sent an exquisite 30-yard lob over the stranded Mathers and into the net.

Deuchar was too young to have seen the legendary Jimmy Greaves play but said he remembered him from watching the Saint and Greavsie show on Saturday mornings as a kid.

Clutching the match ball to his side and with a look of overwhelmed delight on his face, Kenny faced the assembled press pack outside the dressing rooms after hitting that sixth hat-trick of the season to equal the ex-Spurs striker's long-standing record.

"To be mentioned in the same breath as Jimmy Greaves who scored goals at the top level is an honour," he said. "Jeff Steling at Sky Sports gave me a few mentions toady apparently and he sent my gran a signed photo up which she's chuffed with. I just go out every game and try and score as many as I can. The team is playing well and I've just been lucky to get on the end of things."

Deuchar, who continued to work as a doctor one day a week at Stirling Infirmary, was full of praise for wingers Ryan Baldacchino and Gavin Skelton and strike partner David Bingham as well as the management at the club.

Gaffer Rowan Alexander revealed that Deuchar had been skipping in training to get him running on his toes – and 36-goal Deuchar admitted he was terrible to begin with.

"I'm getting better every day. Hopefully it will get me on my toes so I can get in front of defenders and react quicker. Some of the lads have been staying behind after training knocking balls to me to help me improve. I've still got a way to go before I'm the finished article."

Gretna then required just a point to claim the Third Division Championship after a 2-0 win at East Fife that was more emphatic than the score line suggested.

In the first minute Deuchar headed narrowly wide from a Baldacchino cross and after sixteen minutes Ryan McGuffie was unlucky to see his powerful header from a Gavin Skelton corner cleared off the line by Gavin Beith.

The opening goal came on 24 minutes when Chris Innes headed a Steve Tosh cross into the net.

With five minutes left of the first half Baldacchino hit a shot from the edge of the box that crashed back out off the post.

Gretna added the second on the hour when good build up between Deuchar and Bingham set up Skelton who blasted in from 15 yards.

Gretna might have added to their tally when subs Derek Townsley and David Graham went close in the dying minutes.

The club won the silverware the following week and skipper Andy Aitken was in seventh heaven after putting Gretna on their way to celebration as they took the title in style by thrashing Stenhousemuir 7-0 at Raydale.

The hardworking central defender had already seen a header ricochet back off the foot of the post before he climbed to head in Gavin Skelton's free kick after 30 minutes for the opener.

"I'm always pleased to score any goal, but to get the first against Stenhousemuir was fantastic. That's my third winner's medal and your career is so short that it's great to win some silverware."

Aitken said that it had been an honour to wear the captain's armband at Gretna, but felt his job had been made easier by the quality of players around him.

"The experience that we've got in the side with players like Chris Innes, Steve Tosh and David Bingham makes it easy and there should be eleven captains out there on the field anyway. We've just got to go on and try and get as many points as we can now and hopefully get some young boys played as well."

Stenhousemuir had seen Paul McGrillen flash a low shot just past the post as they came out determined to wreck the party, but once Aitken had struck, the floodgates opened.

Four minutes later Skelton fired a tremendous 18-yard volley over keeper Willie McCulloch that crashed up into the roof of the net off the underside of the bar.

And five minutes later top scorer Kenny Deuchar hit a superb third. Ryan Baldacchino jinked across the Warriors' box and Stevie Tosh touched back into the path of Deuchar who unleashed a fierce drive from the angle of the area that rocketed into the top corner. It was his 37th goal of the season and one of the best he'll ever strike.

The hot-shot Doctor netted again in the 59th minute when strike partner David Bingham sent him clear and he held off a challenge before crashing low into the corner.

Deuchar repaid the compliment just two minutes later when his header put in Bingham who coolly went around the keeper and slid number five into the net.

Deuchar almost grabbed a seventh hat-trick of the season to break Jimmy Greaves' record when Bingham again sent him clear in the 66th minute but when McCulloch saved his low shot, sub Bryan Gilfillan was on hand to fire in the rebound.

Andy Smith pounced to net the seventh with eight minutes to go when Ryan McGuffie mis-hit a shot from the edge of the box and the veteran targetman span to sidefoot in from close range.

It was Smith's third Championship medal and completed his own unique treble.

The 36-year-old striker had won the First, Second and Third Division titles and scored in each of the games that sealed the silverware.

"I've got the full set now," said Smith as the celebrations got underway.

"I played and scored in games to win Championships at Dunfermline and Raith Rovers before and I got a wee break in the box today. It's nice to be scoring goals in Championship winning games at my age and it keeps my personal record going."

The jubilant players cracked open the bubbly on the pitch after the final whistle as the ecstatic fans surrounded the tunnel area and the celebrations began in earnest.

Assistant boss David Irons praised the professionalism of the team after they had taken the Championship in emphatic style.

"One of the biggest things we've taken out of this season is how professional the players have been, the manner they've approached each game and gone out and ran over the top of teams. Obviously, it's a full-time club but I think the biggest thing is the attitude and they've shown a great attitude throughout the season," he said.

"It's nice to win a medal and it's something you look back on at the end of your career. There are some players here that have won medals before and some haven't. It's just brilliant for the club, the manager and for Brooks."

There was no let up the following week as David Bingham crashed in a hat-trick in a 6-2 win at Elgin City. But modest Bingham claimed his third was an own goal by Stuart Cumming.

The striker's treble strike took a wicked deflection off the defender its way into the net, but Bingham shrugged that if it was being offered, he'd take it.

"It wasn't a hat-trick – the third was an own goal. But I suppose I'll take it if it's being awarded to me," he said.

"The ball wasn't on my strong side and I just tried to hit the target. Whether it was going in or not before the deflection I don't know. It was quite clearly an own goal but if they have given me it then fair enough."

He had a great chance to add a fourth from the penalty spot but could only cringe as keeper Keiron Renton saved his placed shot.

"I've never scored as many before in a season so I'm quite happy," said 34-year-old Bingham. "My previous best was 22 with Forfar and I scored 19 and 17 with Livingston. I've played at Second Division level before and scored goals there, so I don't see why I can't continue to do so next season. The club's ambition is to get up the leagues. And it's always better to strengthen the team when you're at the top."

Bingham won the SPFA Third Division Player of the Year title form his fellow professionals after being nominated along with team-mate Kenny Deuchar.

Gretna had opened the scoring in the fifth minute at Borough Briggs when Steve Tosh showed great vision to pick out Ryan Baldacchino, who sent in a teasing cross for Kenny Deuchar to thump a header past the helpless keeper.

Elgin levelled six minutes later as Baldacchino was robbed in the middle of the park, allowing Martin Harty to set Willie Martin free and the City striker shrugged off two challenges before slotting the ball under Alan Main.

Gretna hit back and went in front after a superb team move. Tosh picked up the ball just outside the Elgin area and fed Baldacchino, whose touch laid the ball on a plate for Bingham who, with a drop of the shoulder, had time to pick his spot and find the back of the net, sending Renton the wrong way.

The Borderers hit Elgin with a sucker punch by increasing their lead in first half stoppage time. City failed to react to a quick throw on the right, and as a result Bingham was bale to pick out Gavin Skelton on the overlap and the winger took his time before slamming the ball into the net.

Gretna added number four within two minutes of the restart as Skelton and Deuchar combined well by teasing and tormenting the City defence before creating the opening for Bingham, who took full advantage to beat Renton from 25-yards.

It was five a few minutes later when Bingham got in behind the defence and his deflected shot crashed into the net. He then missed from the penalty spot and from the resulting clearance Elgin hit Gretna on the counter attack. Outnumbering them two to one, Adam Nelson unselfishly laid the ball on for Martin who struck it beneath Main for his second.

Mark Birch saw an effort cannon back off the post before Gretna added a sixth when sub Derek Townsley ghosted in at the back post to flick a Baldacchino corner beyond the stranded Renton.

Gretna lifted the Third Division trophy and dedicated it to brave defender Lee Maddison, who had been battling and beating cancer all season, after a 1-0 win at home to bottom club East Stirling.

The popular former Dundee and Carlisle United left back watched on from the stands as skipper Andy Aitken held the Championship trophy aloft. Maddison, 32, was diagnosed with non-Hodgkin's lymphoma the previous summer and had to face up to the toughest challenge of his career.

Right back Mark Birch said: "Even though Lee hasn't been playing this season everybody still sees him as part of the squad. He's a lovely character and the life and soul of the dressing room. We like to keep him involved."

A thirty second pyrotechnic burst and an explosion of black and white streamers filled the sky as Aitken lifted the silverware, but there had been few fireworks on the pitch during the game.

Ryan Baldacchino's 15th minute strike proved enough to ensure that the Borderers finished with a 100% home record. Just a minute after Gavin Skelton had clipped the 'Shire bar with a cross-shot, Ryan McGuffie played in to Baldacchino who beat his marker and fired a low left foot drive across keeper Derek Jackson and into the bottom corner from 18 yards.

But the expected goal avalanche did not arrive as basement boys 'Shire battled and scrapped and the Champions missed a number of chances.

Top scorer Kenny Deuchar was looking to add to his 38-goal tally and thought he'd added number two a minute after the break when he headed in a Mark Birch cross, but was frustrated as he was pulled up for a push and booked for his efforts.

Jackson then clawed away McGuffie's point blank header and Stevie Tosh pulled a shot wide from the edge of the box. Then Deuchar held off his marker and thumped in a powerful drive that Jackson did well to beat away. With six minutes to go Baldacchino touched a free kick to Birch who smashed a 30-yard screamer towards the top corner but Jackson was again equal to it, turning the shot away at full stretch.

In the final game of the season Gretna travelled to Coatbridge and their bid to smash Hearts' long-standing Scottish goal record fell just two short as they thumped five past Albion Rovers.

The Edinburgh side hit an amazing 132 back in 1958 and Gretna required a huge seven on the day to equal that, falling just short as veteran Andy Smith had one chalked off for offside and his team-mates saw a number of chances flash inches wide.

Hard-working midfielder Ryan McGuffie sparked the goal spree in the 23rd minute when he slid the ball into the net at the back post after David Bingham's shot had been half cleared. Rovers keeper Chris Fahey denied Deuchar and Bingham thundered a shot past the post before Gavin Skelton added number two five minutes before the break. Ryan Baldacchino and Derek Collins combined to play in Skelton who turned and fired home instantly from 15 yards.

Fahey scrambled across goal to turn a Baldacchino free kick around the post before the winger got his name on the score sheet in the 55th minute with a cross from the right that deceived the keeper and curled into the net.

It was all one-way traffic as dejected Rovers, who had been told during the week that they would all be released from their contracts after the game, failed to trouble Alan Main in the Gretna goal.

Baldacchino grabbed his second and took his season's tally into double figures in the 63rd minute when his swerving 20-yard free kick found the back of the net through a melee in the goalmouth.

McGuffie wrapped up the scoring in the 75th minute when he pounced to fire home after Fahey had parried out a Deuchar header.

The Champions finished the season with 130 goals for, a goal difference of +101, the only 100% unbeaten home record in Britain, dropped just 10 points away throughout the fantastic campaign and finished twenty points clear of second-placed Peterhead, setting a 98 point record that may never be broken.

Four

Season 2005/06

Champions & the magic of the Cup

VIV BUSBY played alongside George Best, Rodney Marsh and Bobby Moore in the legendary flamboyant Fulham side of the 1970s.

He turned out beneath the Twin Towers in the FA Cup final at Wembley against West Ham in '75. And, although he was obviously disappointed as Fulham went down 2-0, Viv says he remembers vividly the day he took part in the English showpiece final.

"I managed to eat my breakfast though I was obviously nervous," said Viv. "Getting the bus down Wembley Way was fantastic. The fans were lining the road all the way down. The buses then went under the stadium and we went to our dressing rooms."

"We went out and looked at the pitch and got interviewed as the stands were starting to fill up. When we were kitted up and ready to go on for the match there was a slope up onto the pitch and as you were walking up you could see the pitch, the stands were full and the noise was incredible."

The roar of 100,000 fans as he stood on the turf and stood in line to be presented to the visiting dignitary, the May sun beating down as he flicked his long hair out of his eyes, moving his legs on the spot with eagerness to get on with the game.

"I wanted to remember the whole day and I soaked it up. The whole build-up had been great, doing interviews, having pictures taken with models…some of the lads froze up a bit but I felt great and was really up for it," said Viv.

Little did Gretna know at the time that they would have their own special Cup final memories by the end of an extraordinary season.

Striker Viv enjoyed a playing career in football's halcyon heyday and also turned out at Wycombe, Luton, Newcastle United alongside Malcolm 'Supermac' MacDonald, Norwich,

Stoke, Sheffield United and Blackburn Rovers. Like many of the top players of his time, including Pele and Karl Heinz Rummenigge, Viv went out to the United States and had a spell in the NASL with Tulsa.

He also experienced Cup shocks, twice suffering heartache after being dumped out of the competition by non-league sides. He was in the Newcastle team beaten by Hereford – Ronnie Radford's screamer and John Motson's excited commentary – and the Stoke team beaten 3-2 (he scored both goals) by Blyth Spartans, who advanced into the fifth round and were ultimately knocked out by a last-minute corner retaken four times by Wrexham.

Viv was charged with unearthing future talent at Raydale in his role as Academy Director at the club and had spent four years as Denis Smith's assistant at York City. He was then Smith's number two at Sunderland for nearly five years until 1992, and the following year he was appointed manager of Hartlepool United.

After a spell as assistant manager at Sheffield United, Busby became first team coach under Howard Kendall.

The vastly experienced Busby had also been in management at Greek club Ethinkos, Fulham and Swindon. But the enduring image of Busby is of him hanging perpetually in the air in perfect balance, bearded and long-haired, thumping a header past Jim Montgomery as he scrambles across goal in old black and white photographs with a heaving crowd holding their breath in anticipation of the ball rippling the net.

Ten-man Gretna crashed out of the Bell's Cup after extra-time in a cracking five-goal encounter against Morton at Cappielow in a thrilling start to the season between the two favourites for the Second Division title..

The Borderers had fought back from a goal down to lead just two minutes into extra time, but a double from deadly Derek Lilley sent them spinning out after skipper Chris Innes had been shown a red card.

Gretna began well and Morton keeper David McGurn had to be on his toes to beat away a Kenny Deuchar header before Derek Townsley saw another header blocked just minutes later.

Gavin Skelton then had a shot deflected inches wide as Gretna's lively spell continued.

But Morton went one up in the 31st minute with a fine, flowing move that saw Andy McLaren and Jim McAlister combine to feed Lilley who bent his shot into the net from fifteen yards.

Davie Nicholls fired in a sensational leveller in the 67th minute. Ryan Baldacchino beat McLaren down the right and slipped inside to David Bingham who nutmegged Jason Walker and midfielder Nicholls, picking up the ball thirty yards from goal, strode forward and drilled a thunderbolt into the net.

In the dying minutes of the ninety, Lilley went unpunished when he appeared to head butt former Morton man Derek Collins, which sparked a four-man bust up as tempers flared.

Just two minutes into extra time Gretna went in front when Bingham flicked on and hit-man Kenny Deuchar looped home a header.

But soon after Innes was booked for clattering into Walker and then dismissed for tugging at Peter Weatherson's shirt.

Walker equalised in the 109th minute and Lilley popped up with the winner five minutes later when Alan Main parried a McAlister shot at full stretch and the former Leeds and Dundee United man was on hand to put away the loose ball.

Gretna added more experience into the squad as they signed 34-year-old striker James Grady. He had been released by Dundee United and was a target of Motherwell, St. Mirren, St. Johnstone and Partick Thistle but put pen to paper on a two-year deal at Raydale.

He didn't have long to wait to make an impact as he netted on his debut in a 5-1 demolition of Forfar at Raydale, with David Bingham instrumental against one of his former clubs.

Bingham performed like King Midas with everything he touched turning to goals - scoring one and having a hand in the other four as Gretna opened their Second Division campaign in style.

The Borderers unfurled their Third Division Championship flag before kick-off and should have been celebrating the opener in the 14th minute. Kenny Deuchar's brilliant turn and shot forced keeper Colin Meldrum to palm away one-handed and Gavin Skelton fired the rebound over the bar with the goal at his mercy.

Just two minutes later they were stunned as Jamie McQuilken mis-controlled an awkward ball and Barry Sellars left Alan Main wrong-footed with a low drive from distance that flew into the bottom corner.

But Gretna hit back in the 24th minute when Bingham was sent tumbling in the box by defender David Dunn after a flowing four-man move and Ryan McGuffie coolly slammed in from the penalty spot.

And Bingham took just two minutes to put Gretna in front with a piece of sublime individual skill, drifting across the Forfar box and lifting an exquisite chip over the keeper and into the net.

Deuchar added the third in the 36th minute when Bingham played in Skelton whose shot was deflected into the path of the Gretna goal machine to sweep in from close range.

Davie Nicholls flashed a fierce 20-yard drive inches over and Bingham left the Loons' bar vibrating with a cracking volley as Gretna dominated.

Skelton then saw his deep in swinging cross come back off the post and Deuchar's powerful follow-up header came down off the underside of the bar for Ricky Waddell to clear desperately off the line.

But Gretna added number four in the 74th minute when Bingham played in sub Grady, who signed just two days previously, who span and fired home across the keeper.

The influential Nicholls completed the rout two minutes later when Bingham's cross was headed out only as far as the ex-Falkirk man who pulled the trigger and hammered a low volley from 18-yards through sub keeper Neil Ferrie's legs and crashing into the net.

But after such a dominating win, Gretna laboured to a 2-1 victory at Albion Rovers in the CIS Cup First Round in mid-week with a less-than vintage display.

Gretna went ahead in the sixth minute when Kenny Deuchar headed home Ryan Baldacchino's left wing corner. James Grady blasted in the second from the edge of the box in the 75th minute and Rovers were rewarded for their hard work in the dying seconds when Ian Chisholm took advantage of defensive slackness to shoot low past Alan Main.

Grady and Deuchar were on target again as the Borderers left it looking bleak for Raith Rovers with a 3-1 success at Starks Park in the League.

Gretna had a scare in the opening seconds when Paul McManus lobbed just inches over, but within three minutes Deuchar had struck the opener and put Gretna in control after Bingham and Baldacchino had combined to put him in.

Steve Tosh made his return from injury and both he and Ryan McGuffie went close before Grady crossed for Deuchar to thump in a header for number two four minutes before the break.

Raith looked sharper at the start of the second period and pulled one back in the 51st minute when Mark Crilly pounced to fire past Alan Main after some more casual defending.

But Gretna quickly restored their two-goal cushion when Baldacchino crossed from the left and Grady netted with a spectacular diving header.

Baldacchino almost added a fourth but was denied by a superb diving save.

The next week James Grady's sensational strike gave Gretna their 22nd successive home league win, 1-0 against Stirling Albion. But the Borderers had to show some steel after they were reduced to ten men when Ryan Baldacchino saw red. The winger was booked twice in six second half minutes for innocuous-looking challenges in a game littered with fouls.

And Gretna boss Rowan Alexander revealed that Baldacchino was not even responsible for the challenge that earned him his marching orders. "The sending off was a joke," said Alexander. "Ryan wasn't the man who fouled the guy and I have video evidence of that – we'll be appealing."

Kick-off was delayed 15 minutes by the tailback from a motorway smash that held up two coachloads of Binos fans. And they must have wished they were still on the road in the opening seconds when Kenny Deuchar headed back Baldacchino's deep free kick and keeper Myles Hogarth had to turn away Ryan McGuffic's powerful header one-handed.

Gretna hit the winner in the 32nd minute. There looked

little danger when Grady received the ball 25 yards from goal, but with a burst of speed he created the opening and smashed an unstoppable drive whistling into the top corner of the net for his fourth goal in four games. He should have added a second just two minutes later when Bingham's clever flick put him clear, but he dragged his left foot shot wide from 10 yards. And Gretna passed up another great chance in the 38th minute when Deuchar's overhead kick sent McGuffie surging clear but the hard-working midfielder had his head in his hands as he shot wide with just Hogarth to beat.

Alan Main was almost left red-faced right on half time when Paul Hay let fly from distance and the ball squirmed through the experienced goalkeeper's grasp and came back off the post.

Baldacchino went close in the opening seconds of the second period, sliding to meet Deuchar's cross but Ross Forsyth cleared off the line and in the 57th minute he saw a wicked cross-shot deceive Hogarth and come back off the crossbar.

In the 63rd minute Baldacchino slid to tackle Dunn and clearly connected with the ball but was booked for his efforts and six minutes later Paul Hay was left in a heap and, to general disbelief, Baldacchino was sent for an early bath when the ball went out of play.

Stirling almost snatched a point in the 75th minute when David Turnbull towered to head Andrew Graham's cross off the angle of bar and post.

In midweek, Mark Burchill's solitary strike proved enough for SPL Dunfermline to complete a smash-and-grab raid at Raydale in the CIS Cup second round.

But Gretna could hold their heads up high after they dominated against the Premier League side and were only the width of the woodwork, a goal-line clearance and a hotly disputed penalty appeal away from levelling.

The Second Division leaders gave the Pars a mighty fright on a night of lashing rain under the floodlights in a Cup cracker that will have impressed watching Celtic boss Gordon Strachan.

The black and whites signalled their intent as early as the fifth minute when Kenny Deuchar raced onto Aaron Labonte's misplaced header and forced keeper Bryn Halliwell to fingertip his low shot around the post.

Gretna bombarded the Dunfermline goal with a succession of corners before Steve Tosh slipped in Deuchar who went to place his shot past the advancing Halliwell, but the keeper saved with his feet. Halliwell was then out bravely to block at the feet of the inrushing Ryan McGuffie and Ryan Baldacchino, who was proving a real handful for the Pars defence, blazed his follow up over the angle. With Gretna well on top, a defensive slip up in the 17th minute cost them dearly. Jamie McQuilken gifted possession to Darren Young who bore down on the Gretna goal and drilled in a low shot that Alan Main dived to palm away one-handed, but Burchill was on hand to side foot the loose ball into the net from 12 yards.

The Pars would have only one further shot on goal in the entire 90 minutes.

McQuilken almost atoned for his mistake in the 25th minute when he came agonisingly close to finishing off a flowing four-man move. Tosh nutmegged his marker and picked out James Grady who beat the full-back and played in to David Bingham. He teed up the inrushing full-back whose fierce swerving low drive whistled just past the post with Halliwell beaten at full stretch.

In the 30th minute Tosh's in swinging free kick caused panic in the Pars defence and Derek Townsley was unlucky as his thumping volley cracked off the crossbar and over.

And right on half time Gretna had a massive penalty appeal waved away when a goal-bound shot clearly struck a defender's hand following another Baldacchino corner. Gretna continued to take the game to their SPL opposition after the break and Bingham almost levelled in the 57th minute. Baldacchino's corner was flicked on and Bingham shaped to crack a fierce volley at the far post that flashed past the helpless Halliwell, but Lee Makel headed off the line.

With the heavy rain glinting in the floodlights gleam, Gretna's players, their shirts stuck to their skin, continued their relentless onslaught. But Dunfermline stood firm and threw bodies in the way, blocked shots, niggled into fouls and pumped the ball upfield where Chris Innes or Townsley collected and played into feet once again.

With nine minutes to go sub Davie Nicholls was teed up by

McGuffie. Halliwell flung himself full stretch across goal in a despairing attempt to reach the fierce 25-yard drive that looked top corner bound all the way, but flashed just inches over the angle. Gretna crashed out of the CIS Cup, but Dunfermline's relief was palatable at the final whistle.

Gavin Skelton came off the bench to snatch a point for Gretna in their league match against Ayr United at Raydale on the Saturday – and the Borderers were just the width of the woodwork from completing an amazing fightback. With the last kick of a bruising game, Ryan Baldacchino whipped in a free kick from the right and Kenny Deuchar's glancing header hit the post.

It would have been rough justice on an Ayr side who had given the Second Division leaders a mighty fright by racing into a two-goal lead. The Honest Men were quick into the tackle and content to thump long balls forward for their keen front-runners to chase. They went in front in the 23rd minute with free kick straight off the training pitch after Ryan McGuffie had fouled Gareth Wardlaw. Andy Essler played it in low and Paul Hyslop helped it on for Wardlaw who fired in a shot that the diving Alan Main parried, but the spinning ball looped up and dropped into the net, to the joy of the large travelling support. And they were celebrating again just three minutes later when Douglas Ramsey curled in a free kick and Chris Robertson powered a header into the bottom corner. Gretna piled on the pressure after the break and keeper Mark McGeown twice had to be at his best to save from Deuchar.

Gretna pulled one back in the 66th minute when Skelton's corner caused chaos in the Ayr box. McGeown parried Andy Aitken's near post header through a crowd of bodies and David Bingham's flick was headed off the line before Derek Townsley bundled in from close range, which sparked a 19-man melee in the back of the net.

Skelton pounced to poke the leveller into the net from 8 yards with just ten minutes to go when Chris Strain got Steve Tosh's inswinging cross caught up under his studs. Bingham flashed a volley over from a Baldacchino cross before hit-man Deuchar's last-gasp header hit the post – and Ayr breathed a sigh of relief.

Gretna then moved three points clear at the top after a superb defensive display left closest rivals Morton frustrated in a 2-0 success at Cappielow. Goals in each half from Kenny Deuchar and Ryan McGuffie silenced the bumper crowd and sent the travelling support into raptures. Morton began brightly and Ryan Harding headed wide from a John Adam corner but Gretna looked solid at the back with Derek Townsley, skipper Chris Innes and Andy Aitken in top form. The Borderers went ahead in the tenth minute. Innes pumped a high ball into the box and when Morton failed to clear, Townsley did well to square for Deuchar to pounce and fire into the net from close range for his sixth of the season. Morton's Jim McAllister then flashed an angled volley over and Chris Millar fired a 20-yard drive that Alan Main held at the second attempt as the 'Ton looked to level. But Gretna were just inches from adding a second when David Bingham's header from a Gavin Skelton corner went just wide. In the dying seconds of the first half Alex Walker was unlucky when his powerful 35-yard drive thundered out off the underside of the bar. Morton piled forward in search of an equaliser after the break, but for all their possession they never really posed a threat as Gretna worked hard to break down their attacks. And the win was sealed ten minutes from time when Ryan Baldacchino sent over a corner and McGuffie rose at the near post to send a powerful header ruffling into the net for number two.

Partick made their first trip to Raydale and James Grady thought he'd silenced the Jags boo-boys with a stunning diving header to put Gretna 2-0 up – but Thistle hit back and salvaged a point with a last-minute penalty.

Former Firhill hit-man Grady chose to sign for the Borderers over a return to the Glasgow side in the August and had taken some stick from the large travelling support before he finished off a fine flowing move just four minutes after the break. David Bingham nutmegged Darren Brady in the middle of the park and Ryan McGuffie ran on and played a great ball into the path of Ryan Baldacchino who fired in a first-time cross for Grady to send a superb diving header crashing into the top corner of the net. Gretna had started well and in the opening minute Bingham played in Gavin Skelton down the left to fire in a dangerous low cross that William Snowdon hooked clear only as far as Steve Tosh who sprayed it wide for Baldacchino, Kenny Deuchar heading his centre over the bar. Alan Main had to be on his toes in the 12th minute, parrying over a bending Richard Gillies free kick as Thistle looked a well-organised unit who passed the ball around neatly.

Five minutes later Skelton crossed from the left and Deuchar powered to the near post but guided his volley just wide. In the 28th minute Tosh played a long ball up to Deuchar who controlled and fired in a 25-yard drive that Kenny Arthur got down well to save, but it looked the wrong option with Baldacchino free down the right screaming for a pass.

Three minutes later Gretna did work the ball out to the winger who hung up a cross and as Deuchar challenged, Arthur spilled the ball and Bingham coolly side footed into the net from 12 yards.

Right on half time Sean Kilgannon bent in a brilliant quickly-taken free kick that Main turned around the post at full stretch as Thistle continued to look a threat. Just two minutes after Grady had netted the second, Thistle were gifted a way back into the game when a defensive slip left Jukka Santala free to head into an empty net. In the 70th minute Baldacchino crossed and Skelton flung himself into a goal-bound diving header that was blocked by Grant Murray and with ten minutes to go sub Davie Nicholls smashed in a 22-yard free kick that Arthur parried away superbly at full stretch.

In the dying seconds Gretna won a corner that was cleared and at the other end Derek Townsley's loose header put in Jimmy Gibson and as the big centre half raced back and slid to tackle, Gibson went down and the ref had no option but to point to the spot. Kilgannon stepped up and kept his cool to smash the spot-kick low into the bottom corner.

Gretna got back to winning ways the following week with a comfortable 3-0 win at Alloa.

An early header by Derek Townsley and late goals by Chris Innes and Ryan McGuffie saw the Borderers continue their impressive away form.

Gretna dominated the opening exchanges and capped their flying start with a goal when Townsley headed Gavin Skelton's corner into the net.

David Bingham then had a shot tipped over by Alloa keeper Gary McGlyn, who also did well to block an effort by Steve Tosh. Gretna keeper Alan Main made a couple of good saves to deny Alloa late in the first half, with Jose Quitongo and Andy Brown both going close.

Kenny Deuchar blasted wide for Gretna early in the second half and Skelton was also off-target before Alloa enjoyed their best spell, although Main was rarely troubled. Gretna again assumed the upper hand with Skelton forcing McGlyn into a fine save, before Deuchar headed against the post with ten minutes remaining. A minute later, Gretna increased their lead when skipper Chris Innes forced home Baldacchino's corner and then two minutes from time, Deuchar and sub David Graham both had shots blocked before McGuffie blasted the loose ball into the top corner of the net.

Steve Tosh's early strike then ensured that Gretna stayed top of Division Two as they dominated at home to Dumbarton. Tosh struck after just four minutes when he fired low into the net from the edge of the box after a neat one-two with Kenny Deuchar.

The margin of victory should have been much greater but a combination of complacency, poor finishing and dogged defending by the Sons kept the score down.

The Raydale men almost doubled their lead in the seventh minute, but Ryan McGuffie was inches away from connecting to James Grady's low delivery across the face of goal.

The Dumbarton defence were all at sea and Deuchar wasted a glorious chance three minutes later when he shot wide from 10 yards after being set up by David Bingham.

Sons keeper Stephen Grindlay then had to dive low to his left to claw away a downward header from McGuffie after a perfect cross from Gavin Skelton. Ryan Baldacchino then raced down the right after being fed by Grady, but the tricky winger shot inches beyond the far post. Dumbarton survived another scare in the 37th minute when Craig Brittain hooked the ball off the line after Grindlay mis-judged a back-header from Deuchar. Gretna continued to dominate in the second half but failed to add to their tally due to a combination of poor finishing and some frantic defending from the visitors. Dumbarton began to weather the storm for a period as they limited rampant Gretna to a couple of long-range efforts from central defenders Chris Innes and Andy Aitken.

James Grady then hit his fifth of the season and captain Chris Innes was also on target as Gretna maintained the only unbeaten record and top spot in Division Two with a 2-0 success at Peterhead. It was Gretna's first victory at the Balmoor Stadium in seven attempts and their fourth consecutive away win.

Gretna were on top from the kick-off and went in front in the eighth minute. A poor back pass from Iain Good fell to Grady and the hit-man finished in style, firing into the net off the left-hand post from the edge of the penalty area. Andy Aitken had been booked after 15 minutes and he was carried off with a knee injury after landing awkwardly seven minutes later. Steve Tosh went close to adding a second and Derek Townsly headed just over before an excellent tackle by Jamie McQuilken denied Martin Wood at the other end.

Despite facing a strong wind in the second half, Gretna continued to take the game to the Blue Toon, who had been promoted with them in the summer. The points were wrapped up with a simple second on the hour. Ryan Baldacchino sent over a pin-point corner kick from the left and Innes rose unchallenged to power a header into the net from the edge of the six-yard box.

The excellent away form continued with a 3-1 win at Forfar as two last quarter goals took the points at Station Park, but Gretna were made to fight all the way for the win.

Former Gretna striker Martin Cameron cut in from the right for a shot on the run in the third minute before Gretna forced two corners in quick succession at the other end. From the second Derek Townsley put Kenny Deuchar through only for his shot to cannon out off the underside of the bar. Forfar keeper Francois Dubourdeau then saved James Grady's low 25-yard effort.

Gretna's pressure paid off in the 17th minute when Steve Tosh fired against the upright and Deuchar was onto the rebound to make no mistake from five yards.

Darren Gribben equalised just after the break when he unleashed an unstoppable 25-yard drive into the top corner. Forfar's tails were up and two minutes later Cameron pounced on an Alan Main fumble, but Townsley cleared his effort off the line.

A minute later Gribben cut in from the left and fired another shot across Main's goal. Gretna hit back and after Tosh and Townsley had gone close, they went ahead in the 74th minute. Skelton's shot looked to be skidding wide until Chris Innes' deflection wrong-footed Dubourdeau and the ball span into the net. Jon Voigt replaced Cameron in the 80th minute and almost levelled just a minute later, Skelton clearing his effort off the line. Deuchar added his second late on, rising above the tiring Forfar defence to head in a Tosh free-kick and maintain the four point cushion over Morton.

In midweek, it wasn't the prettiest goal he'd ever scored, but Kenny Deuchar's fiftieth in a Gretna shirt would live long in his memory. Deuchar silenced the critics who said he couldn't cut it in the Second Division as he maintained his phenomenal strike rate in a five-goal romp over Raith Rovers at Raydale. And with a bit of luck, Deuchar could have been celebrating a hat-trick as fourth-placed Raith were blown apart. He was punching the air in delight in the 42nd minute when he got on the end of James Grady's low cross and his deflected shot span inside the near post, beating sprawling keeper Ally Brown to put Gretna 3-1 up.

Earlier Ryan McGuffie had cut the Raith defence open with a penetrating run and pass that that left big hit-man Deuchar clear, but he raced on and fired wide from the edge of the box with just the keeper to beat. And five minutes after the break McGuffie's clever reverse pass put in Deuchar and Brown got down well to smother his low shot.

Strike partner James Grady was also in blistering form, netting a superb double to keep neck and neck with Deuchar in the scoring charts.

Derek Townsley had already smashed a 30-yard drive inches over the bar before he pounced to put Gretna in front in the tenth minute, heading in Gavin Skelton's deep free-kick from a narrow angle at the far post. And with Gretna turning on the Champagne style, it wasn't long before they doubled their advantage.

David Bingham, playing just behind the front two, sprayed a brilliant ball out to Ryan Baldacchino and Deuchar unselfishly nodded back his pin-point centre for Grady to fire in a volley from 8 yards.

With torrential rain lashing down, Raith went close as Todd Lumsden glanced a header just past the upright from a Scott Crabbe corner. And they pulled one back when Willie Lyle beat Skelton down the right and crossed to the far post for Laurie Ellis to stoop and thump home a low header.

Gretna got back in control and McGuffie made another strong run and squared to Grady whose first time drive was brilliantly palmed away one-handed by Brown who was diving the wrong way.

Rovers were reduced to ten men in the 53rd minute when Crabbe was shown red for an ugly two-footed lunge on McGuffie that so incensed the Gretna players that Grady was booked as they surrounded the striker.

Baldacchino's pace and skill was tormenting Rovers and a Tosh bending shot was parried away at full stretch before Townsley fired just over as Gretna looked to make their advantage count.

Tosh added number four, the hard-working midfielder lashing a low left foot drive into the bottom corner when Skelton's cross was only half cleared.

And Grady completed the rout in the 71st minute. The former Dundee United ace added his second when his close control flicked up Bingham's low shot and he span to crash in a low volley that gave Brown no chance. Grady headed a Birch cross just wide and Brown had his fingers stung in making good saves to deny Skelton and sub David Graham as Gretna moved seven points clear at the top.

Ryan Baldacchino then fired in an injury-time 40-yard special as a 3-1 win over Morton at Raydale took that lead to ten points. The tricky winger spotted keeper David McGurn off his line after the Morton stopper had raced out to head away from

Kenny Deuchar when David Bingham sent him clear. Baldacchino controlled and, from just outside the centre circle, sent a spectacular chip dipping into the net past the back peddling McGurn and a desperate defender.

The former Carlisle ace raised a finger in salute as he was hoisted into the air by Steve Tosh and mobbed by the rest of his ecstatic team-mates. "As soon as I hit it, I knew it was in," said Baldacchino afterwards. "I try it in training every day but it was still nice to see it come off in a game."

It was the perfect response after Morton had pulled one back out of the blue in the 89th minute when Scott McLaughlin crashed a stunning, dipping 25-yard volley into the bottom corner.

Gretna were well worth the three points after a classy display that left 'Ton reeling on the ropes. James Grady robbed David MacGregor and whipped in a centre for Deuchar to glance in a header that McGurn saved down low in the 16th minute as the game started at a frantic pace.

And with man-of-the-match Tosh making some brilliant tackles and moving the ball around the pitch fluently, Bingham fired a right-foot volley just wide from 20-yards.

Morton's approach was more direct and a long ball bounced over the defence but Kevin Finlayson rushed his shot and dragged into the side netting from a narrow angle.

Gretna came out guns blazing after the break and Deuchar out jumped McGurn but his flicked header fell wide and Bingham rifled one just past the post. In the 57th minute MacGregor was booked for taking down Baldacchino and Morton were punished when Skelton flighted in the free kick for skipper Chris Innes to power a far post header into the net.

Ten minutes later Alan Main made a superb double save, denying hot-head sub Andy McLaren and as the ball broke free Derek Lilley looked certain to score but Main outstretched a leg to save.

At the other end Grady took a quick throw to Deuchar who played on for Bingham to set up McGuffie with McGurn, his head swathed in bandages after a collision, saving his drive at full stretch.

But McGuffie was celebrating in the 87th minute when Bingham's close control beat his man and he drilled in a low centre for the tireless midfielder to smash in from close range. McGuffie almost added a fourth in the dying seconds when he played in Deuchar whose shot was blocked by McGurn, with the number 8 crashing the rebound against the crossbar.

The great run continued with a 3-1 win at Ayr United, who posed little threat apart from a good spell of pressure in the closing stages. Gretna took control from the start and went in front in the ninth minute when Kenny Deuchar netted with a spectacular diving header from a Derek Collins cross. Shots from Gavin Skelton and James Grady went close before Gretna went two ahead in the 27th minute as Steve Tosh's intended cross from the right wing deceived keeper McGeown and landed in the net.

Ayr almost pulled one back in the 39th minute when Chris Wardlaw's 20-yard effort was cleared off the line by Tosh.

Gretna assumed control again after the break with Deuchar clean through on goal but when he appeared to be brought down in the box the ref waved play on. Gretna's third came in in the 57th minute when Chris Innes stole in unmarked to fire in at the back post after good work by Tosh.

Ayr got back into it and Wardlaw headed wide when it looked easier to score, but they pulled one back in the 74th minute as Raymond Logan lashed in Paul Hyslop's cut back. Ayr had further chances but Alan Main was on top form to deny the Honest Men.

Gretna then blew a three-goal lead at Partick as the Jags staged an amazing late fight back to share the spoils at Firhill.

Thistle dominated for the opening twenty minutes of the game with Jukka Santala and Graham Dorrans going close before Gretna took the lead in the 22nd minute.

David Bingham set up Kenny Deuchar who saw his shot blocked by keeper Stewart but Ryan McGuffie followed up to net from close range.

Gretna improved after the break and increased their lead in the fiftieth minute when Deuchar out-jumped Stewart and headed down for Chris Innes to stoop and head home. It was the centre back's sixth goal in eight games.

And the Borderers looked home and dry in after 72 minutes when Deuchar ran on to a through ball and slipped a shot low past Stewart.

When Jags sub Stephen McConalogue scored with a looping shot after 82 minutes, it looked to be a mere consolation, but then his fellow sub Billy Gibson pulled another back in the 85th minute and alarm bells started ringing.

Graham Dorrans pounced on a defensive mix-up to fire home the leveller with just two minutes to go.

The club had a break from League duty with a tricky trip to Edinburgh-based East of Scotland side Preston Athletic in the First Round of the Tennent's Scottish Cup and they cruised through with a comfortable 6-2 win at Prestonpans.

Gretna went one up in the tenth minute when David Bingham set up James Grady whose low shot beat keeper Gilpin from 12 yards.

The lead was doubled in the 18th minute when Grady span to volley in a Skelton throw from the angle of the box. The game was effectively over two minutes later when Derek Townsley headed home a Ryan Baldacchino cross from the left.

Gretna were soon on the attack again after the break with Davie Nicholls going close to adding another. Grady is the little striker with the big grin - and his smile was beaming broader than the Tyne tunnel

on the hour as Baldacchino played him in to complete his first hat-trick for the club from close range.

Two minutes later good play between Tosh and McGuffie set up Kenny Deuchar for a close range strike that flew in and within three minutes David Bingham added the sixth, again from close range.

Subs David Graham and Danny Grainger came close to increasing Gretna's tally before defensive slackness let in Phil Hobbins for Preston's first after 87 minutes and just before the final whistle Sean McAuley added a spectacular second to make the scoreline more respectable.

James Grady continued his hot goalscoring form as he fired in a 20-yard wonder strike to move Gretna 11 points clear at the top of the table in a 4-0 win over Alloa at Raydale.

Grady picked his spot and bent a stunning shot into the top

corner from the edge of the box for the goal that put Gretna on the road to victory.

Further goals from strike partner Kenny Deuchar, Ryan McGuffie and Mark Birch were the icing on the cake in a comprehensive win.

Raydale Park observed a minutes' silence for the legendary George Best before kick-off and the atmosphere in the ground remained subdued until the 16th minute when Derek Townsley's towering net-bound header from Gavin Skelton's corner hit the unlucky Grady and deflected wide with keeper Gary McGlyn sprawling.

Three minutes later Ryan Baldacchino's driving run was halted by Steven Learmonth and the ball broke to Grady who cracked in the unstoppable opener.

Balacchino set off on another jinking run three minutes later and played a neat one-two with Grady before smashing in a low drive that John Ovenstone cleared off the line.

McGuffie was desperately unlucky not to add a second in the 34th minute when he let fly with a 30-yard screamer that flew past McGlyn but crashed back out off the inside of the post.

Gretna did add number two five minutes later when Skelton crossed from the left and Deuchar rose majestically to power a header into the bottom corner as Gretna dominated.

Alloa's Ross Hamilton was left cursing his luck just after the break with a drive that flashed just wide, but it was the closest the Wasps came to stinging the League leaders.

Grady's pace took him clear of Richard Walker and he sent over a great cross from the left that the inrushing McGuffie headed wide from a good position in the 64th minute.

But the hard-working midfielder made amends for that miss just six minutes later when David Bingham chipped to the far post and he nodded down and into the net between the keeper and the post.

Birch added the fourth with six minutes to go after a strong run when his cross-cum-shot from a narrow angle flew over McGlyn's head and bounced in off the far post.

Gretna's relentless promotion push rumbled on with a 3-0 win over Peterhead - but Blue Toon winger Graeme Sharp was left cursing the Raydale woodwork.

Sharp had his head in his hands as he saw a both a powerful header and a curling shot come back off the Gretna crossbar in the first half.

But goals from the deadly trio of David Bingham, Kenny Deuchar and James Grady maintained the Borderers unbeaten start.

Gretna went in front in the 16th minute when Grady's clever ball split the Peterhead defence and Ryan Baldacchino pulled the ball back from the bye-line for Bingham to fire into the bottom corner of the net.

But the Highlanders weren't about to roll over and they hit back when Keith Gibson curled a free-kick over the wall and Alan Main dived to parry away at full stretch, Sharp drilling the rebound into the side netting.

Mark Birch then denied Bobby Linn with a superb last-ditch tackle before Allan Youngson curled in another free kick that saw Sharp's header rattle the bar.

Gretna went two up three minutes later when Baldacchino whipped in a centre and Deuchar powerfully got in front of keeper Paul Mathers at the near post to crash in a header.

Steve Tosh then embarked on a driving run, beating two men and setting up Grady who screwed his shot wide.

Right on half time Sharp was again unlucky when he curled in a shot that crashed off the bar.

Deuchar almost doubled his tally after the break when he span his marker and fired in a low shot that Mathers dived to turn around the post.

Gretna sealed the win in the 71st minute when Bingham released Skelton who fired in a low shot that Mathers parried out and Grady was on hand to lash in the rebound.

Peterhead were reduced to ten men in the 77th minute when Chris Heggerty was sent for an early bath for a second yellow card.

James Grady then struck twice and left the ground clutching a magnum of bubbly for his man-of-the-match display as Gretna shattered tough-tackling Cove Rangers dreams of a Scottish Cup shock with a 6-1 mauling in the Second Round.

The hitman also picked up a bottle of whisky before kick-off as the player of the month for the Annandale Observer.

But Grady revealed that he wouldn't be savouring the win with a festive tipple - as he doesn't touch a drop. "I'm teetotal!" laughed Grady. "The whisky will go to the mother-in-law and the Champagne to my grandfather. It was a tough game and we've got a few scratches and kicks, but everyone has come through unscathed, which is the main thing."

Grady was celebrating the opener after just two minutes when Davie Nicholls' through ball split the defence and he raced on to round keeper Ivor Pirie and roll into the empty net.

Cove were defending in numbers and getting stuck into some heavy challenges but Gretna went two up in the 14th minute when Ryan McGuffie raced down the right and centred low for Kenny Deuchar to ram in from close range.

With the Cove goal under siege Deuchar hooked a volley just wide, a last-ditch block denied McGuffie and Grady glanced a header just over.

But in the 32nd minute Cove put together a three man move and Gary Clark cut in from the left and drilled a low 20-yard drive into the bottom corner.

Kevin Tindal then scythed down Grady and Gretna were amazed as ref Alan Boyd waved play on. Raydale was in disbelief again four minutes later when Ryan Baldacchino crossed and Grady's powerful header was tipped onto the underside of the bar with Deuchar forcing in the rebound, only to be denied by a late linesman's flag.

But Derek Townsley did add the third on the stroke of half time when he headed in a Baldacchino free kick at the far post.

The powerful driving runs of Steve Tosh were almost rewarded a minute after the break when Scott Fraser hacked his shot off the line.

Tosh embarked on another surging run in the 63rd minute, Tindal handling his net-bound flick with McGuffie stepping up to smash the resultant penalty into the top corner.

Grady grabbed his 15th of the season in the 77th minute when he smashed into the roof of the net at the second attempt and Nicholls hit the goal of the game with eight minutes to play. He let fly with a thunderous 30-yard drive that flew in off the foot of the post. Gretna were drawn away to First Division St. Johnstone in the Third Round draw after the game.

James Grady was again on target in a 1-0 win at Dumbarton before Forfar's Darren Gribben hit a double to shatter British football's only unbeaten League record as Gretna went down to a shock 2-1 home defeat on Christmas Eve.

The Forfar striker bent in a first half free kick and fired a 35-yard wonder strike to clinch it for the Loons.

Gretna's James Grady had fired just wide and Gavin Skelton saw a volley saved by keeper Francois Durbourdeau before Gribben hit the opener in the 29th minute.

He curled a free kick over the wall from 20-yards and the low sun dazzled Alan Main's eyes, causing him to lose the flight of the ball, and it ended up in the back of the net.

Gretna levelled a minute before the break when Mark Birch played a one-two with Grady and fired in a low centre that the unlucky Alan Rattray bundled into his own goal.

Gretna - who had been unbeaten at home since April 2004 - never really got going but Durbourdeau pulled off a great save from a Ryan McGuffie header ten minutes after the break.

If Gribben's opener was fortuitous, his second in the 70th minute was class. He spotted Main off his line and smashed the winner into the top corner from long range.

Five minutes later Derek Townsley let fly from 25 yards but Durbourdeau was equal to it, turning the ball over the bar. And with Gretna getting increasingly desperate as the clock ran down, the French stopper was again the Forfar hero as he finger tipped a McGuffie drive around the post.

Ryan Baldacchino had been forced to limp off early on in the game when he pulled up and felt pain in his knee, but didn't realise at the time that his medial ligament had completely detached. He would be out, save a handful of games, for the rest of the season.

Baldacchino's red-hot form had stirred an interest at the Maltese F.A., for whom he qualified to play through a Sta Venara-born Grandfather, now residing in Sliema on the Mediterranean island.

He had already had a call-up to International football in 2003 when: "They spoke to me after I made them aware I was eligible through my grandparents and great-grandparents," said Baldacchino.

"The MFA called me up and left it with me to sort out. I spoke to the embassy and they told me I would qualify for a passport but the MFA would have to put it forward to speak to them as a special case."

"I'd love to get called again - even just to go over and train and the MFA could have a look at me - but it would be even better to play in a full international," said the former Bolton, Blackburn and Carlisle star.

"Last time, I was disappointed to miss out in the friendly against Kazakhstan, but hopefully my form over the last few seasons has warranted another call-up."

"It would be absolutely fantastic for both me and my family to see me pull on the Malta shirt, especially for my grandfather. I would obviously be very willing to play and hopefully I could add something extra to the team."

Record signing David Graham got off the mark and set up two more as he ran Ayr ragged in a tough game that saw both sides reduced to ten men as Gretna got back on track with a 3-0 win at Raydale.

Full back Mark Birch unselfishly handed Graham the ball when Gretna were awarded a last minute penalty and the former Stranraer ace made no mistake from the spot, firing home low for his first for the club.

Graham made his first full start for Gretna, coming in for the injured Baldacchino, and he had keeper Mark McGeown diving to save a shot in the opening seconds.

In the ninth minute his pace got him free down the right and he centred for David Bingham to cleverly flick over a sliding defender with his left foot and crack in a right foot volley that the keeper parried wide.

Davie Nicholls then sent Kenny Deuchar clear but McGeown stood up well and blocked his low drive with his feet.

In the 29th minute Ryan McGuffie was booked for clipping a defender late as he cleared but within a minute the midfielder had been flattened off the ball by Raymond Logan, who was shown a straight red.

Gretna made their advantage count as they went in front four minutes before the break when Graham embarked on a brilliant solo run at pace from the half way line and pulled back for James Grady to sidefoot into the roof of the net past a defenders' desperate lunge.

Nicholls twice came close right on half time, flashing a volley onto the roof of the net, then forcing McGeown into a brilliant diving save with a fierce drive.

McGuffie was sent off for a second yellow card in the 54th minute following an innocuous-looking foul on Craig Conway.

Grady's brilliant ball then sent Bingham clear but McGeown saved as he went to slide a shot past him.

Gretna had to endure a nervy ten-minute spell as Alan Main saved with his feet from Cashmore's low drive and safely gathered Jerome Vareille's follow-up volley.

Cashmore then whipped in a dangerous cross and Derek Townsley's headed clearance beat Main and cannoned off the angle of post and bar.

But in the 82nd minute Graham got into the Ayr box and unselfishly poked a cross into the path of sub Dene Shields, just back from a loan spell at Stranraer, and he fired into the net from close range.

Graham got on the scoresheet himself when Steve Tosh's free kick struck Mark Casey's elbow in the wall and referee MacDonald pointed to the spot.

Gretna then marched into the fourth round of the Tennent's Scottish Cup with a commanding display at First Division St. Johnstone, a solitary Steve Tosh goal winning the game. On the performance, Rowan Alexander's men could well have been mistaken as the team from the higher Division.

Goalkeeper Alan Main didn't have one direct shot to deal with in the entire ninety minutes and was restricted to collecting crosses, which he dealt with impeccably at one of his former clubs.

The only goal of the game came early in the 12th minute as David Graham's electric pace took him to a ball that always looked a defender's one, crossed for Kenny Deuchar to knock the ball into the path of Tosh who drilled low into the net from 12 yards.

Davie Nicholls had a shot blocked and Deuchar was denied by Saints keeper Kevin Cuthbert while at the other end Andy Jackson shot wide from 15 yards.

Gretna continued to press after the break with Tosh and Ryan McGuffie flashing shots across the face of goal, while Gavin Skelton should have done better when set up by Graham.

The closest that Saints came to salvaging anything was five minutes from the end when Jason Scotland shot across goal after a penetrating run.

Gretna's reward for the win was a trip to Clyde in the fourth round after they pulled off one of the great shocks and dumped out Champions Celtic, who had Roy Keane making his hoops debut, 2-1 at Broadwood. The influential David Bingham was missing from the team after picking up a mystery virus, similar to M.E., that would keep him out for the rest of the season.

Gretna maintained their five point lead at the top of the table the following week in a hard-fought match at Morton that saw their closest rivals come back from a two-goal deficit to snatch a share of the points.

With midfielders Steve Tosh and Ryan McGuffie out through suspension, new signings Allan Jenkins from Stranraer and John O'Neil from Falkirk came in to make their debuts for the Borderers.

And Gretna got off to the ideal start with a goal after 11 minutes when Kenny Deuchar rose to head a Gavin Skelton cross beyond the scrambling keeper and spinning inside the post. It was the towering striker's 50th league goal in 50 starts to maintain his incredible scoring record.

Morton were stung into action and Ryan Harding headed across goal and James McAllister had a shot saved by Alan Main.

Gretna added a superb second in the 31st minute when Skelton bounced a throw-in off O'Neil's back and crossed for shaven-headed Chris Innes to smash a spectacular curling left foot volley rippling into the roof of the net from 20 yards.

But Morton were thrown a lifeline five minutes before the break when Derek Lilley headed in a cross from the right.

Deuchar almost restored Gretna's two-goal lead on the stroke of half time, but Stefan Gonet did well to block his close-range header.

Gretna were dealt a blow in the opening minutes of the second half when new boy Jenkins was the victim of a hefty challenge which went unpunished and saw him replaced by Dene Shields.

Andy McLaren went close for Morton before Shields fired just over from a Derek Collins cut back.

O'Neil then had a shot tipped away by Gonet before Alan Main was back in action, turning away a Kevin Findlayson drive.

Morton's pressure told in the 79th minute when Chris Millar headed back across goal for Peter Weatherson to net from close range, sparking mad celebrations. 'Ton went desperately in search of a winner but sub Chris Templeman lashed wide deep into stoppage time.

Steve Tosh and David Graham both hit doubles in the next match as Partick Thistle were hit for six at Raydale.

Gavin Skelton and James Grady also got in on the act as the leaders ran riot.

Davie Nicholls had displayed Gretna's attacking intent with a couple of efforts that flew just wide before the Black and Whites went in front in the 25th minute with a well-worked goal.

Graham got away down the right and fired a cross to the back post where Skelton cleverly nodded back for Tosh to head into the roof of the net from close range.

Tosh almost added a second two minutes later when Nicholls sent him clear but the advancing Kenny Arthur blocked his shot.

Then Arthur turned a fierce Ryan McGuffie drive over the bar following a goalmouth scramble and Derek Townsley headed the resultant corner over and onto the roof of the net as Gretna turned up the heat.

This spell of pressure saw Jags boss Dick Campbell introduce new signing Sandy Hodge for David Craig and Thistle went close a minute later when Paul Ritchie stabbed a Scott McCulloch cross agonisingly wide.

But six minutes later John O'Neil exchanged neat passes with Graham before firing over from the edge of the box.

Within sixty seconds, Graham's brilliant turn in the box earned himself a yard of space and he made no mistake, hammering a low left foot drive inside the near post.

There was no let up for Thistle after the break and in the 50th minute Tosh sent Kenny Deuchar clear but Arthur raced out and saved as the big hit-man went to knock past him.

Then livewire Graham lashed a half volley just over the angle of bar and post as Gretna kept up the pressure.

They were rewarded with a third in the 55th minute when Skelton played in O'Neil who pulled back to Tosh. The midfielder's initial effort was blocked but he followed up to tuck away into the bottom corner.

Thistle debutant Billy Dodds set up Richard Gillies in the 63rd minute, but Alan Main denied him with a one-handed save. Five minutes later Dodds was replaced by Adam Strachan and Will Snowdon came on for Gillies as Campbell shuffled his pack.

But ruthless Gretna went further ahead in the 75th minute as Tosh flicked on for Gavin Skelton to shape and fire a rocket volley into the net, sparking a mass exodus of the large travelling Jags support.

McCulloch hit a consolation with 10 minutes to go when he drilled a shot home following a clever one-two.

Gretna didn't take their foot off the gas and Skelton crossed for sub Grady, who'd only been on the pitch six minutes, to flick a header over the stranded Arthur and into the top corner.

In the last minute Jamie McQuilken chased a lost cause to the bye-line and cut back for Graham to smash in number six from close range.

Gretna marched on with a convincing 3-0 victory at Alloa in an uninspiring game that they never looked like losing against the Second Division's basement strugglers.

Alloa began brightly with Graeme Brown and David McGeown going close before Gretna gradually gained control with John O'Neil and Davie Nicholls having shots blocked in quick succession.

Gretna made the breakthrough in the 28th minute when Steve Tosh's quick free kick was touched on by David Graham to Derek Townsley who scored with a low shot from 15 yards.

Gretna continued to dominate without creating anything clear-cut while Iain Nicholson shot wide at the other end as half time approached.

Alan Main made a good blocking save to deny the inrushing James Stevenson and Gretna's second came on 55 minutes when Graham was tugged back by Hamilton and Ryan McGuffie netted from the penalty spot.

Sub James Grady went close with a diving header before Alloa were reduced to ten men when John Grant was harshly red-carded for a challenge on Tosh, which probably merited no more than a yellow.

Gavin Skelton wrapped up the scoring with a powerful drive in the 81st minute after good work by McGuffie. Morton drew with Ayr, meaning Gretna's lead at the top was extended to seven points with a game in hand.

Gretna had to fight it out in a replay with First Division Clyde as the Tennent's Scottish Cup fourth round ended 0-0 in a game that saw three players sent for an early bath.

Despite the scoreline it was a pulsating Cup-tie with Gretna probably having a slight edge, particularly in the first half when they might possibly have had the tie sewn up.

James Grady and Ryan McGuffie tested Clyde keeper Peter Cherrie in the opening minutes, then at the other end Alan Main dealt easily with an effort by Stephen O'Donnell.

McGuffie and David Graham then had goal-bound efforts blocked before the game exploded in the 29th minute when Gretna skipper Chris Innes and Clyde's Alex Williams were red-carded after a clash in the corner of the Gretna penalty box.

Kenny Deuchar replaced the injured Graham after 36 minutes and Derek Townsley went close before the end of a tempestuous first half.

The pace of the game understandably dropped for the opening 25 minutes of the second half but after that Clyde were seen more as an attacking force.

Main had to be alert in the 78th minute when he beat Craig Bryson to a through-ball to kick clear. The Clyde fans were on their feet three minutes from time when Tom Brighton almost won it with a header that flashed inches wide of Main's right hand post.

Clyde were reduced to nine men in the dying seconds when Chris Higgins received a second yellow card following a late challenge on Deuchar.

Gretna's top League form continued as they beat Peterhead 3-1 at a rain-swept Balmoor with John O'Neil scoring his first for the club.

The leaders were seldom troubled and mastered the tricky conditions much better than the Blue Toon.

The opening half hour belonged to Gretna with Davie Nicholls firing over in the fourth minute and an O'Neil drive from 25 yards forcing keeper Mathers into a fine save.

Shortly after it was almost inevitable when Gretna went in front in the 15th minute when Allan Jenkins played a low ball across goal and O'Neil fired home from 12 yards.

Peterhead levelled very much against the run of play in the 35th minute when Alan Main's clearance into the strong wind cannoned off an opponent and fell to Kevin Nicol who lobbed the ball into the empty net from 25 yards.

The Blue Toon had a good chance just after the break when hesitancy at the back let in Graeme Sharp who shot straight at Main.

But Gretna regained control and O'Neil had a shot deflected for a corner and then Ryan McGuffie had a 25 yard drive tipped over by Mathers.

They went back in front in the 75th minute as Gavin Skelton's cross from the left carried over to McGuffie who hooked into the net from a narrow angle.

Skelton wrapped things up five minutes from the end when he was sent clear by Jenkins and beat Mathers with a fierce low effort.

In Chicago on Valentine's Day 1929 seven men were gunned down in a spectacular mob-hit organised by Al Capone.

Seventy-seven years later in Gretna, James 'machine gun' Grady hammered in a stunning hat-trick to fire the black and white's into the fifth round of the Scottish Cup.

First Division Clyde were left riddled with bullet holes as the Gretna assassin's right boot proved more deadly than a Tommy gun in the fourth round replay.

Gretna went in front in the 25th minute on an ugly night under the floodlights with swirling wind and lashing rain as Steve Tosh played a clever quick free kick into Grady on the edge of the box.

The nippy striker looked to have been forced wide by Steven Masterton but he rode the weak tackle and jinked inside before lashing an angled drive inside the near post giving keeper Peter Cherrie no chance.

Clyde almost levelled when Eddie Malone's long range effort clipped the top of the bar and flew over then Alex Williams shot wide from a great position.

Williams was again guilty of a glaring miss four minutes before the break when Tom Brighton's pace took him clear down the right and Williams completely miscued with the goal at his mercy.

In the 63rd minute Tosh made a vital goal-line clearance to deny Craig Bryson after Williams had set him up.

And three minutes later Gretna sub Dene Shields raced down the left and crossed for Grady to flick beyond Cherrie for Kenny Deuchar to slide in and smash the second into the roof of the net and send the packed ground into raptures.

Within two minutes Clyde were left against the wall when Shields squared to Grady who let fly with a 25-yard drive that flashed into the bottom corner for 3-0.

Clyde were reduced to ten men in the 72nd minute when Craig McKeown slid into a foul to pick up a yellow card and then talked himself into a second from fourth official Martin Sproule, who had replaced ref Dougie McDonald after he fell ill with food poisoning prior to kick off.

And Grady completed his treble in the 81st minute when Ryan McGuffie played him in on the right edge of the box and he calmly picked his spot, drilling low across Cherrie and into the bottom corner of the net.

Brooks Mileson had handed out 100 red roses to the first women through the turnstiles on the night and Grady left the ground clutching the match ball, a magnum of Champagne and a single red rose and joked - I'm off home to score again!

The cheeky striker said: "Have I scored three times on St. Valentines night before? Let's just say I'll be going for a fourth when I get home, that's for sure!"

"I don't know what the missus will think of that, but that's what the red rose is for!"

"It's a wee bit early to say that we can win the Cup, we've got another tough tie with St. Mirren now. They're leading the way in the first division and they'll probably be an SPL side next year, but we've got a chance against anyone at home - we scored four and kept a clean sheet tonight, which was pleasing. A lot was said in the build-up to the game and it fired us up a wee bit. It just goes to prove we are a decent side."

The games kept coming thick and fast and Steve Tosh scored the only goal in a 1-0 win at Raith in the league before the fifth round tie against Saints when Kenny Deuchar headed Gretna into the semi-finals of the competition and said - 'It was a great team effort.'

Deuchar rose to meet Gavin Skelton's 75th minute corner and glance a header across keeper Tony Bullock's full stretch dive and low into the bottom corner of the net just inside the far post. And Raydale erupted. The big number nine reeled away with his arms aloft in celebration and he was leapt on by Ryan McGuffie and Mark Birch.

Deuchar then turned hero at the other end in a nervy last few minutes with two strong tackles as Gretna held out against the First Division leaders to become the first Second Division side to reach the last four in the Cup since Forfar in 1982.

"I can't believe it," said Deuchar afterwards. "We were getting a few chances but nothing clear cut. However, we are always confident we can score, especially at Raydale. We knew if we kept working hard something would have to give and luckily it did. If you had told me at the start of the season we'd be in the semis I'd have laughed at you."

St. Mirren had a strong wind at their backs in the first half and almost went in front in the 14th minute when Gretna's defence failed to cope with a long ball into their area and Charlie Adam fired a low left foot drive across the face of goal and inches wide.

James Grady steered a header past the post at the other end and Deuchar shot narrowly wide. Skelton then saw his fierce drive dip just over the bar as Gretna created the better chances.

Gretna keeper Alan Main was subjected to a constant noisy barrage from the Saints fans behind his goal and he produced a superb save to prevent Adam putting Saints ahead in the 32nd minute, re-adjusting his feet and arching back to tip over the on-loan Rangers' man's deflected drive.

After the break Gretna were unlucky when Chris Innes powered in a header from a Skelton corner that Derek Townsley turned in a the post but was flagged for offside.

Bullock then produced an equally spectacular save after Grady's tremendous skill to keep up the ball twice and bounce on two headers to beat his marker before firing in a top-corner-bound volley that the keeper turned over one-handed.

Mark Birch drove a free kick narrowly wide and Grady's long-range effort flew straight at the Saints keeper.

In the 74th minute quick-thinking Gavin Skelton span his man and, spotting the Saints keeper off his line, almost caught him out with a wind-assisted dipping 35-yard drive that the back-peddling Bullock bundled around his post. Skelton bent in the resultant corner and Deuchar met the ball at the near post with a glancing header across the keeper for the winner.

After Deuchar's strike, John Sutton wasted Saints' best chance to equalise when he dragged his shot across the Gretna goal after hard-working Adam had set him up.

The players and management were mobbed by shell-shocked fans on the pitch at the final whistle.

Gretna goal hero Kenny Deuchar is the man in the white coat…so no-one would be coming to take him away when he said Gretna were just ninety minutes away from the possibility of European football.

The fully-qualified Doctor said: "I've never regretted my decision to come and play football. I still work as a doctor one day a week and the manager has been good letting me do that. I wouldn't be able to play football if the club didn't let me do that. Obviously I've worked too hard to get that qualification to let it all slip away. The club have been good to me and hopefully I'm now repaying them."

"The prospect of European football is definitely a big carrot to dangle in front of any player. To be 90 minutes away from something like that…it's obviously something we need to play for but we still need to win on the day. We need to go out in the semi final and work hard and I've no doubt we'll do that."

"But now we need to get back to concentrating on the league because we want to be promoted and that's the most important thing."

There was no sign of a Cup hangover on the Tuesday night as five different players were on target for the Borderers in a 5-0 romp at freezing Forthbank.

Stirling Albion had won eleven of their previous thirteen league games, but were put to the sword by a rampant Gretna.

The Black and White's started the game strongly and James Grady and Kenny Deuchar had both gone close before they went in front in the 32nd minute, just when Stirling were starting to get into the game.

Grady collected the ball on the left edge of the area and drove forward to plant a precise low shot beyond Myles Hogarth.

Any hopes Stirling had of boosting their play-off hopes were shattered after the break as Gretna piled on the goals with some clinical finishing.

Gavin Skelton grabbed the crucial second in the 52nd minute with a cracking strike that flew in off the post after he'd been set up by a Grady back-heel.

Two minutes later the game was effectively over. Steve Tosh floated a free kick into the area from wide on the right and, when the ball was nodded down, central defender Derek Townsley pounced to net from close range.

Albion tried to hit back and Paddy Connolly sent an effort just wide after springing the offside trap, then sub Robert Dunn almost put away a Dougie Wilson cross.

But Gretna, who were now 11 points clear of Morton at the top, were largely in command and Allan Jenkins cracked in a crisp 20-yarder for his first goal for the club in the 72nd minute and five minutes later Ryan McGuffie wrapped things up when he tucked away from six yards.

Gretna went 14 points clear without ever finding top gear in a 3-0 win over Dumbarton the following mid-week.

The Sons packed men behind the ball, were hard working in midfield and used an offside ploy to frustrate the leaders.

But with the visitors sat so deep, they rarely troubled Alan Main at the other end and were content to break up Gretna's play on a dreek night.

In the 12th minute Allan Jenkins sent Stevie Tosh clear down the right and when his low centre was deflected into Ryan

McGuffie's path, the midfielder drove in a low shot which was blocked on the six yard line.

Tosh limped off to be replaced by Ryan Baldacchino and the winger unlocked the Sons stubborn defence for the opener ten minutes later, playing a one-two with McGuffie and racing to the bye-line to cross for the unmarked James Grady to power a downward header looping over the diving Stephen Grindlay's outstretched hand and into the corner of the net.

Gretna upped the tempo after the break and took just six minutes to stretch their lead. Grady slipped a ball through to strike-partner Deuchar who went around the sprawling Grindlay and, from a narrow angle, saw his side-footed shot deflected against the post by a defender on the line with the ball squirting across the goalmouth for the inrushing McGuffie to fire in despite getting in a tangle with a desperate in-sliding defender.

Two minutes later Jenkins was sent sprawling in the box but Gretna's appeals for a clear-cut looking penalty were waved away by the referee.

It was 3-0 in the 62nd minute as Grady fired over a deep far post cross from the left and the unmarked Deuchar powered a header rippling into the back of the net.

Jenkins then showed great technique on his home debut to flash in a 25-yard volley that proved too hot to handle for Grindlay, who gathered at the second attempt, and hit a volley just over from a half-cleared corner.

Main kept his fifth successive clean sheet in the final minute with a great diving save from a curling effort by sub Andy Rodgers.

But a late double from Morton's Chris Millar then condemned Gretna to only their second defeat of the season.

The 'Ton winger raced onto a Derek Lilley flick-on and lobbed the advancing Alan Main for the opener in the 78th minute at Raydale. And he applied the sucker punch two minutes later when he tucked away a low James McAllister cross.

Gretna almost pulled one back immediately with James Grady unlucky as his 18-yard drive crashed off the crossbar with keeper David McGurn well beaten.

Strike partner Kenny Deuchar found the net in the 89th minute when his low drive from a Ryan Baldacchino pull-back deflected off the heel of the in-sliding Peter Weatherson, wrong footing McGurn and spinning into the corner of the net. But second-placed 'Ton held out to claw the gap back to 11 points.

Gretna started brightly and almost went in front in the tenth minute, Grady crossing for McGuffie to ram in a shot from 8 yards that McGurn brilliantly parried away at full stretch.

But both defence were on top for long spells of the game, Derek Townsley just failing to connect with Baldacchino's whipped in free kick before the break the next real chance.

Mark Birch picked up a knock and was replaced by John O'Neil at the interval with Davie Nicholls moving into the back three.

Townsley again went close in the 49th minute with his towering header from a Skelton corner flying straight into the grateful McGurn's arms.

O'Neil then cleverly beat his marker and fired in a fierce 25-yard drive that McGurn spilled but recovered to punch away as Deuchar was set to pounce on the loose ball.

Gretna were given a warning shot when a mix-up at the back saw Lilley through on goal but Nicholls made a great recovering tackle to deny the 'Ton hot-shot.

Morton almost added a third in the 85th minute when Weatherson played in sub Jason Walker whose shot was blocked by Main, with Nicholls blocking Weatherson's follow-up drive.

But Gretna bounced back and took another step towards securing the title with a good 2-0 win away to Partick Thistle the following week.

Gretna dominated proceedings and went in front in the 41st minute when Kenny Deuchar tapped in after Kenny Arthur had saved brilliantly to deny Gavin Skelton.

Deuchar added the second in the 73rd minute when Tosh played him in and he outpaced Scott Boyd before calmly sliding the ball past a despairing Arthur.

Ryan McGuffie then struck twice in the final minute in a 4-2 win at Somerset Park as Gretna were made to fight all the way by a lively Ayr side battling for Second Division survival.

Gretna controlled the opening stages and deservedly took the lead in the 20th minute when Steve Tosh crossed from the right for John O'Neil to fire in a low shot.

The lead lasted only seven minutes when slack defending allowed Jerome Vareille to run through and beat Alan Main with a low shot from 15 yards.

Gretna went back in front after 38 minutes when James Grady's right wing cross was volleyed into his own net in spectacular fashion by James McKinstry.

Just before the break Conway out paced Mark Birch but fired into the side netting.

Ayr came out all guns blazing after half time but Gretna weathered the storm and Davie Nicholls and Kenny Deuchar both went close at the other end.

Ayr refused to lie down and some more sloppy defending saw Main forced to smother a Varielle shot on the line. Derek Townsley and Ayr's Gareth Wardlaw were booked in the melee that followed.

Ayr's pressure paid off when they were awarded a penalty for handball in the 86th minute. Craig Conway fired the spot-kick past Main and a share of the spoils looked likely as the seconds ticked away. But in the final minute, never-say-die Gretna regained the lead when Gavin Skelton crossed from the left and McGuffie volleyed in to devastate United.

From the kick-off McGuffie regained possession and was chopped down as he weaved his way into the box, before picking himself up to dispatch the fourth from the penalty spot.

Steve Tosh smashed in a superb double to clinch the Second Division Championship on the Saturday and proved he's the man for the big occasion.

He struck twice from corners as Gretna came back from behind to beat Alloa 2-1 and sparked a Raydale party.

Tosh had also netted a spectacular overhead kick to seal the Third Division title the previous season and beamed: "That's two years in a row I've scored the goal to win the Championship. To be fair, other boys have scored every week, but I'll take the praise when I can."

Boss Rowan Alexander was hoisted onto the player's shoulders as the celebrations began at the final whistle.

But Gretna went behind to a shock opener in the second minute when they failed to deal with a high ball and Jamie Stevenson crashed an angled shot across keeper David Mathieson and into the bottom corner from 12 yards. It almost got worse sixty seconds later when Stevenson let fly from the edge of the box with a drive that flashed just past the angle of bar and post.

Basement club Alloa again went close four minutes later when Robert Sloan crossed to the near post and Paul McLeod's powerful effort was brilliantly turned over by Mathieson as the Wasps kept up the pressure.

Gretna's attack was lacking it's usual punch with Alloa quick into tackles and moving the ball smartly around the park, with assistant boss Davie Irons an animated character in the dug-out as he attempted to spur on the leaders.

In the 42nd minute John O'Neil headed on and Dene Shields span and hooked a good chance across the face of goal.

But the Raydale crowd was lifted as the tannoy announced Ayr taking the lead at title rivals Morton and 30 seconds later Derek Townsley headed Gavin Skelton's corner into the path of Tosh and he smashed a tremendous shot high into the corner of the net from 20 yards.

Gretna hit the winner in the 67th minute when O'Neil's deep corner was headed back by Townsley and Tosh again let fly with a low left foot drive from 20 yards that crashed into the net.

Relegation-haunted Alloa continued to press forward and forced a succession of corners as Gretna endured some nervous moments.

In the final minute Skelton cleared Michael Bolochoweckyj's powerful downward header off the line and the Borders took the title at the final whistle with six games to go as closest rivals Morton blew it and went down 4-0.

And so the club made its way to Hampden Park to face First Division Dundee in the semi-finals of the Tennent's Scottish Cup as Champions. Just thirty seconds before half time in the biggest game in Gretna's history, hit-man Kenny Deuchar latched onto a defensive mistake by Dundee, side-stepped advancing keeper Kelvin Jack and slid a low left foot shot goal wards from a narrow angle.

Bobby Mann raced back and hooked the ball away with Deuchar bouncing with his arms in the air in celebration. The crowd held it's collective breath as the referee glanced towards his linesman then gave the goal. And the stands erupted as a sea of black and white went crazy.

Gretna had been comfortable throughout the half, probing away from midfield and moving the ball around the superb emerald green surface of the national stadium. Keeper Alan Main had spread confidence throughout the back-line, comfortably catching anything that the Dens Park side pumped into the box.

The Dark Blues came out after the interval with renewed vigour, but Gretna never once looked troubled.

And the stuffing was knocked out of them in the 58th minute when Ryan McGuffie jinked into the box from the right and was sent tumbling to the turf by a lunging foul from Mann.

McGuffie dusted himself down, faced away from the goal and span to fire the spot-kick low past the diving Jack and rippling into the bottom corner of the net before he was mobbed by his ecstatic team-mates.

More celebrations were sparked in the 82nd minute when sub Jamie McQuilken went down the left and drilled in a dangerous low cross that was deflected into the net by the outstretched leg of Barry Smith past the wrong-footed Jack.

While the Dundee fans began streaming out of the stadium, Gretna's stayed on long after to hail their Hampden heroes as they danced and sang on the touchline, hoisting boss Rowan Alexander into the air, pulling owner Brooks Mileson into tight bear hugs as the party continued long into the night.

Midfielder Davie Nicholls said afterwards he felt Gretna could do a 'Crazy Gang' and pull off a shock against the mighty Heart of Midlothian in the final.

The classy midfielder's appearance in the semi had been his first at Hampden in his long and eventful career.

And Nicholls, 34, was so excited at the prospect of turning out on the hallowed turf that he was up and dressed at the club's hotel at 5.45am on the morning of the fixture.

Nicholls compared Gretna's amazing run to Wimbledon's in the FA Cup in the 1980s when they went all the way and beat favourites Liverpool to lift the silverware.

"We can only go out in the Cup final and give it our best shot," said Nicholls.

"But I can think back to Liverpool v. Wimbledon in the FA Cup final all those years ago. No-one gave them a hope of winning yet look what happened. That's why we've got to go out and give it our all."

"If we can maybe get a little bit of luck then you never know what can happen. But for a Second Division club to get to the final is an unbelievable achievement. I'm delighted for Brooks because he is a genuine, down-to-earth fella."

And midfield playmaker Steve Tosh admitted he had been dreaming about scoring at Hampden in bed on the Friday night.

"Before the game I was talking to James Grady and I said 'How many did you score when you were dreaming last night, wee man?' He just laughed but I think I got two, Gavin Skelton got three or four and all the other lads hit the net with a couple as well!"

Tosh grinned at the prospect of Gretna playing in the UEFA Cup the following season and said: "The prospect of Europe? What about the prospect of missing Magaluf and Clarky's stag-do? It's surreal but to play in a Scottish Cup final means everything to the players now."

There was no let up in the celebrations as young Gretna hitman Matthew Berkeley came off the bench to grab his first senior goal as the Borderers cruised to a 3-1 win over third-placed Peterhead in the League.

Sub Berkeley, who had been recalled from a loan spell at Conference North club Workington just a week before, pounced to head in from a corner in the final minute.

Despite the efforts of a defender to hook the ball away off the line, it crashed into the roof of the net to leave the 18-year-old with a huge grin on his face.

"No-one's taking that one away from me," he said. "The lads in the dressing room have been winding me up that it was an own goal, but everyone knows it was mine. I enjoyed my spell at Workington and I'm in good form at the moment."

Gretna went in front in the opening minute when James Grady's shot was deflected into the path of Jamie McQuilken, who fired in at the back post from close range.

In the 12th minute Peterhead only half cleared a corner and Gretna new boy Scott Paterson fired in a fierce volley from 16 yards that keeper Paul Mathers parried away spectacularly at full stretch.

But the Blue Toon levelled on the half hour when Paterson was booked for a deliberate hand-ball in a dangerous position on the edge of the box, and Gretna were made to pay when Douglas Cameron bent the resultant free kick over the wall and into the back of the net from 20 yards.

Gretna went 2-1 up in the 69th minute when McQuilken and Grady combined to slip in substitute Dene Shields, who sent a low left foot drive crashing inside the near post.

And Berekeley, who'd only been on the pitch eight minutes, wrapped things up in the dying seconds when Gavin Skelton whipped in a corner and he flicked in a header that deflected off a defender and was rifled into the roof of the net by another.

Inspirational midfielder Steve Tosh then slapped on the gloss with a devastating first-half hat-trick as Champions Gretna shattered the Second Division points record with a 6-0 massacre of Stirling Albion - the previous record being held, ironically, by the Binos.

Tosh painted the town red with a sensational display after pleading with manager Rowan Alexander not to rest him for the fixture against play-off hopefuls Albion and left Raydale Park with the matchball tucked under his arm.

Gretna fielded a vastly experienced side with seven players over thirty on the pitch and regulars Kenny Deuchar, Ryan McGuffie and Mark Birch on the bench.

Stirling were given a warning in the fourth minute when Gavin Skelton let fly from 30 yards with a swerving drive that clipped the top of the bar.

Tosh was clearly enjoying himself and in the 27th minute cheekily nut-megged danger man Paddy Connolly with a ball back to Scott Paterson. A minute later he was celebrating the opener after Allan Jenkins' ball into the box was cleared straight back to him and he played in the inrushing Tosh who lashed into the roof of the net from an acute angle.

It was 2-0 in the 38th minute when Stirling didn't clear a corner and John O'Neil's clever back-heel put in Tosh who calmly side-footed in low inside the near post.

Within sixty seconds Tosh set up James Grady who smashed an angled shot across keeper Myles Hogarth and into the bottom corner of the net for 3-0.

Grady then span himself to the ground in attempting to play a pass and lay prostrate for several seconds before giving a little salute to the bench with a grin as Gretna's 'Crazy Gang' ripped Albion apart.

On the stroke of half time Jamie McQuilken raced down the left and pulled back for Skelton to roll the ball into the path of Tosh who passed his treble low into the net from 12 yards past the despairing Hogarth.

Just after the interval Tosh drove into the box and poked back to O'Neil who touched on for McQuilken. He was pulled back by a defender, but poked into the corner of the net off-balance for the fifth.

Tosh came off to an ovation as McGuffie replaced him and Deuchar came on for Grady.

In the 73rd minute a McQuilken cross was spilled by Hogarth and O'Neil prodded a shot goal wards that was cleared off the line by a defender.

Sub Dene Shields wrapped things up with three minutes to go. O'Neil dribbled across the box and played in Deuchar who blasted against the post, before ramming the rebound against Hogarth's legs with Shields slipping in the loose ball.

After such a devastating display it was a shock as Gretna turned in a strangely inept performance to go down 2-1 at Forfar Athletic who were desperately trying to avoid being sucked into the relegation play-offs dogfight.

Gavin Skelton was denied by keeper Murdoch early on but Forfar went in front in the 8th minute when the nippy Andy Jackson, on-loan from St. Johnstone, broke clear to beat David Mathieson with a low shot.

Mark Birch came to Gretna's rescue with a last-ditch tackle to foil Lombardi but in the 31st minute indecision by Scott Paterson let in Jackson to volley home number two.

Forfar had chances to increase their lead early in the second half as Davie Nicholls cleared in a goalmouth scramble and Ritchie Montgomery headed wide with the goal at his mercy.

James Grady pulled one back from the penalty spot in the 73rd minute following a handball but Forfar could have added another when Jackson saw his point-blank header parried away by Mathieson.

Skipper Chris Innes and Ryan McGuffie hit the net in a 2-0 success at Dumbarton before Gretna were presented with the Championship trophy at the end of the final home match of the season as they beat Raith Rovers 2-1.

Chris Innes headed over the top from a Steve Tosh corner and David Nicholls tried his luck from range before Kenny Deuchar latched onto Todd Lumsden's slack back-pass to fire home the opener in the 8th minute.

Lumsden made amends before half-time blocking a Deuchar shot on the goal-line and heading a fierce effort from John O'Neil over the bar.

Battling Raith levelled in the 54th minute when Chris Silvestro placed a shot past Alan Main after Paul McManus cut back the ball from the bye-line.

And Rovers could have gone in front two minutes later but Main blocked from Laurie Ellis after Innes left a back-pass short.

But man-of-the-match Gavin Skelton hit the winner in the 74th minute. David Graham sent Ryan McGuffie down the right flank and he crossed for Skelton to stab in at the second attempt after Alistair Brown had blocked his first shot.

James Grady almost made it three when he turned past two markers to hammer a shot past Brown only for it to come back off the inside of the post.

Brown produced a great save to turn Tosh's goal-bound effort round the post late on and Emilio Jaconelli came close at the other end with an overhead kick that flew over the bar but Gretna were not going to be outdone and the party started at the final whistle with the players spraying Champagne on the podium as they were presented with the silverware.

But the Champions then went down to a shock 2-1 defeat at Stirling Albion on the final day of the season.

Stirling took the lead in the 21st minute when Chris Hay took advantage of a defensive mix-up on the corner of the penalty area, rounded Alan Main and slotted the ball into the net.

And just before half-time, the Binos made it two when Steven Boyack released Paddy Connolly and, although Main blocked his initial effort, Stirling's top scorer nodded in the rebound.

It was a different story after the break as Gretna dominated.

Myles Hogarth made excellent saves from Kenny Deuchar and Chris Innes and substitute David Graham missed a good chance before Deuchar pounced from close range after a goalmouth scramble with 18 minutes left.

In injury time, Hogarth made a brilliant stop to deny Deuchar and John O'Neil received a second yellow card for knocking in the rebound with his arm.

The Borderers bounced back and mighty Hearts were given a huge scare in the Tennent's Scottish Cup Final as Gretna took the Premier League runners-up to extra time before going down in a nerve-wracking penalty shoot out at Hampden. It was tough justice on the Second Division champions who had walked out tall onto the national stadium turf and left with their heads held high after a battling performance. With a huge following of 12,000 roaring on underdogs Gretna from the stands, Hearts started well and were unlucky in the sixth minute when Mark Birch charged down a Takis Fryssas shot and from the rebound Deividas Cesnauskis hit a low drive past Alan Main that came back off the post.

But Gretna held firm and refused to be dominated by the Tynecastle giants. In the 26th minute Gavin Skelton let fly with a bending free kick that was flying towards the top corner with keeper Craig Gordon displaying all his International class to fingertip over at full-stretch.

Hearts went in front in the 39th minute when Robbie Neilson launched a long throw into the Gretna box and when skipper Chris Innes just managed to get a glancing header away from a challenging striker, Rudi Skacel shaped to fire an angled low left foot drive across Main and into the corner of the net.

But Gretna refused to lie down and battled back after the break with midfield schemer Stevie Tosh firing a low shot into the side netting. Sub David Graham injected some pace into the Gretna attack and he was desperately unlucky not to level when he weaved through Jambos defence before rounding keeper

Gordon. As he shaped to shoot into the empty net, Neilson raced back to deny him with a superb sliding tackle.

Gretna had their tails up and levelled in the 74th minute. Cesnauskis lunged in on John O'Neil as he went into the box and sent the Gretna midfielder tumbling. Ryan McGuffie stepped up and fired the spot-kick low to Gordon's right but the keeper guessed right, diving to parry. The ball span back into the in-rushing McGuffie's path and he made no mistake, ramming in the rebound to send the Gretna contingent into raptures.

Gretna looked the only winners at this stage and created another great chance in the 84th minute when a cross fell to Innes at the back post but the unlucky central defender didn't connect cleanly with his volley and held his head in his hands as it bobbled harmlessly wide.

But the game went into extra time and Skacel went close to winning it for the Champions League-bound Capital side with a shot that smacked off the post. Hearts hot-head Paul Hartley was then sent off near the end for petulantly kicking out at Derek Townsley.

As the game went to the lottery of a penalty shoot-out, Pressley, Neilson, Skacel and Pospisil hit the net with their kicks for Hearts. James Grady and Birch fired in for Gretna, but Gordon saved Townsley's kick as he changed his mind at the last moment and Gavin Skelton, the club's longest serving player, smashed against the crossbar and the fairytale fell just short.

Gretna skipper Chris Innes was obviously gutted to lose the game on penalties – but believed that the club had done enough to silence their critics and prove they deserved their spot in the UEFA Cup.

The towering defender was one of the stars as Gretna refused to lie down to the SPL giants at Hampden and he was looking forward to leading out the team on a European adventure.

"The teams who were challenging for fourth place in the SPL said that we shouldn't be in the competition, but I think our performance at Hampden proved that we were worthy of it," said Innes.

"I was fortunate to play in Europe with Kilmarnock. For Gretna to be in it is phenomenal and it's fairytale stuff. We always seem to create media interest, and who is to say we can't go on a wee run."

The cool defender, whose straight posture, always with his head up, ball playing from the back and strong tackling inspired confidence throughout the team, continued: "How far we can go depends on who you get because I have played against some hard teams you have never heard of." The former Dundee United ace added: "I'm 29 now and maybe have another four or five years left and I'm looking to be at Gretna for the rest of my career."

Five

Season 06/07

The UEFA Cup

Gretna had a pre-season trip to Austria and strengthened their squad during the summer break by adding Irish winger Brendan McGill from Carlisle and experienced midfielder Neil MacFarlane from Aberdeen to the pool.

The Borderers snapped up 25-year-old former Republic of Ireland International McGill on a free at the second attempt, two years after he had rejected the chance of a move to Raydale Park when Carlisle were relegated to the Nationwide Conference.

Dubliner McGill had joined Carlisle from Sunderland in 2001 and he made 194 appearances in five seasons, scoring 22 goals.

He was looking forward to the challenges of the Scottish First Division and was eagerly anticipating the chance to play European football.

"I was delighted to get the chance of a move to Gretna. I'm very fortunate, as I've left one ambitious club to go to another very ambitious club. Gretna are going places and I'm hoping to be part of that," said McGill.

"They've had back-to-back promotions and it's really exciting what could happen here. Never mind what they're doing in the league - there's also the small matter of European competition! That's a great achievement by the club and a real honour for the players."

The club made another major signing as Mick Wadsworth joined the staff as Director of Club Development.

The respected and vastly experienced 55-year-old coach began his new role as the first-team squad returned from their week-long training camp in Austria.

"I'll be using my experience to help in all areas of the club," said Mick, former right-hand man of Sir Bobby Robson. "From the Youth programme through to the first team, I'll be helping

Rowan Alexander, David Irons and David Holdsworth be the best that they can and supporting every department at Gretna FC."

"I've been in discussions with the club for a long time to shape a role that is most beneficial to the club. From looking at players to bring in and broadening that area to helping with the youths, I'll help move Gretna FC forward to bigger and better things," he continued.

"I've known Brooks Mileson for 10 years and we've talked many times about working together – I'm delighted it's finally happened."

Wadsworth began his coaching career at the FA in 1985 as a Regional Coach in the North-West of England. He was Official Match Observer of the England national team from 1988-1992 under both Sir Bobby Robson and Graham Taylor.

He had also been a Technical Co-ordinator on the FA's Excellence Programme and had a coaching role with England at the 1990 World Cup, as well as being involved with England U21's and managing the England Non-League team and England Youth team.

Wadsworth had managerial experience at Carlisle United, Scarborough, Colchester United, Oldham Athletic, Huddersfield Town and Portuguese side Beira-Mar.

He had been an assistant manager at Norwich City, Newcastle United, Southampton and Shrewsbury Town and had further International experience as national coach at St. Kitts & Nevis and DR Congo.

Gretna manager Rowan Alexander said: "I'm delighted to have a guy of so much experience and expertise on board at Gretna FC so early in the club's growth and development – it's a massive coup for the club."

Gretna Managing Director Brooks Mileson, who had a health scare with internal bleeding during the summer, said: "It is testament to how far Gretna FC has come when we can attract such quality into an extremely important position for both the footballing and non-footballing areas of the club. With Mick's vast knowledge, I'm sure that Gretna FC can only go from strength to strength."

It was business as usual as midfield General Steve Tosh inspired Gretna to a six-goal demolition job with a stunning hat-trick in their Division One opener as Hamilton Academical were shattered at Raydale.

Tosh was like a dynamo all over the pitch, probing around the box with neat passes, surging forward and tackling back. He said afterwards: “I would warn our fans not to expect 6-0 and 5-0 every week. We just hit top form and Hamilton had a bad day.”

Gretna unfurled the Second Division championship flag before kick-off and were in champagne form, also thumping the woodwork on three occasions and having another cleared off the line. The Borderers went in front in the 14th minute when James Grady's slide rule pass put in Tosh and he tucked his shot into the bottom corner after sending the keeper the wrong way from 16 yards.

He almost added a second within 60 seconds when Anthony Stevenson left a back pass short and Tosh nipped in to round the keeper and roll in a goal-bound shot that Derek Fleming cleared off the line. Tosh and Grady combined again five minutes later when the nippy forward's clever back heel put in Tosh, but keeper David McEwan dived to parry away his curling shot.

Tosh struck again in the 26th minute when Hamilton left another back pass short and he took the ball around the keeper and squeezed it into the bottom corner from a narrow angle. Grady was unlucky not to get on the scoresheet three minutes later when he fired a Kenny Deuchar cross against the post.

But he did get his first of the season three minutes before half-time when a brilliant piece of individual skill took him clear of Steven Thomson and he coolly chipped over the advancing keeper and into the net.

A lapse in concentration just 30 seconds after the break by Steven Thomson allowed Steve Tosh to send a first-time half-volley rocketing into the corner of the net for his hat-trick. Tosh then saw a shot clip off a defender and bounce out for a corner off the post. Ryan McGuffie was unlucky not to add to the tally from the resultant flag kick as his header thumped out off the angle of bar and post as Gretna totally dominated.

An awful blunder by Hamilton keeper McEwan gifted Gretna their fifth in the 68th minute. He fluffed a clearance straight to winger Brendan McGill who went round the shot-stopper and rolled the ball into the empty net. McEwan redeemed himself five minutes later with a spectacular full-length dive to fingertip Gavin Skelton's 25-yard drive over the bar.

Gretna completed the rout two minutes from time when substitute Graham capitalised on poor defending by Steven Thomson to cross for McGill who stroked the ball in at the back post.

Former Newcastle United and Livingston forward Colin McMenamin was then signed from Shrewsbury Town on a free transfer. McMenamin began his career at neighbours Annan Athletic alongside midfielder Ryan McGuffie before they both joined the Magpies. McMenamin also had a loan spell at Falkirk in 2003. He joined young Blackburn Rovers defender Craig Barr as the fourth signing of the season.

Gretna drew Irish Eircom League side Derry City in the UEFA Cup 2nd Qualifying Round and had the play the home First Leg at Motherwell's Fir Park as tiny Raydale was not up to European standard.

Derry had beaten Swedish former UEFA Cup winners IFK Gothenburg 1-0 in both legs of the first qualifying round and Gretna knew that they would provide a stiff opposition.

"I had a funny feeling we would get Gretna and I hoped we would because it will be great to meet up with my old mates," said Derry centre back Darren Kelly, a former team-mate of a number of Gretna players at Carlisle United under Roddy Collins.

"I'm looking forward to the challenge of playing Gretna. We know what they have achieved and the progress they have made over the last few years. We will have to give them our respect, but we are worrying about our own corner and we'll be going out with the same belief as we had against Gothenburg," said Kelly.

And Gretna were stunned as a shattering three-goal salvo from the Candystripes in ten second-half minutes left them with a mountain to climb in the second leg of the UEFA Cup tie.

The Borderers got their Euro adventure off to a storming start and took a 12th minute lead but, roared on by a 2,000 strong noisy, flag waving red and white army in the Davie Cooper Stand, the Eircom League side powered back to take a healthy 5-1 lead home to the Brandywell Stadium.

"We got a lesson in how to close people down," said boss Rowan Alexander afterwards.

"I'm very disappointed we didn't match their work ethic, which is something we pride ourselves on. We made it easy for them."

Gretna went in front when Derek Townsley's free kick was flicked on by James Grady to find Brendan McGill on the right-hand edge of the penalty area. The winger intelligently cushioned the ball into Ryan McGuffie's path and he pounced to lash a low left foot volley nestling into the bottom corner of the net for Gretna's first-ever European goal.

Just a minute later, McGuffie just failed to connect with a Grady cross as Gretna moved the ball around crisply.

But Derry hit back in the 22nd minute when they pumped a long free kick forward and Sean Hargan crossed for Darren Kelly to power in a far post header.

Gretna almost went into the dressing rooms with a half time lead as City keeper David Forde stumbled and Steve Tosh went around him but hit the side netting from a very narrow angle.

In the 54th minute skipper Chris Innes was adjudged to have tripped Ciaran Martyn and was shown yellow by the Croatian official. Kevin Deery stepped up and bent a superb free kick into the top corner of the net from 30 yards.

Deery, who had been called up into the Republic of Ireland U21 squad, sent the travelling fans into raptures just three minutes later when he smashed another stunning drive from distance into the top corner.

Gretna were left reeling on the ropes six minutes later as Martyn burst into the box, rounded Alan Main and fired the fourth past two defenders on the line.

The Borderers were shell-shocked and Martyn added the fifth in the 75th minute when he cut through the heart of the defence with another powerful run and blasted home.

With pride battered and bruised by the big, physical Derry side, Gretna would make the journey to Ireland like a wounded animal.

"We gave away silly free-kicks and our passing was sloppy at the back but we have learned a lot tonight. You always learn a lot from defeat," said Alexander.

"It hurts because they did not adhere to what I told them and it is very annoying. We made it easy for them because we didn't play the football that we know we can. If we had matched their work ethic and closed down people then maybe the quality would've shone through."

Gretna put the disappointment of the heavy UEFA Cup defeat behind them with a hard-fought 2-1 victory over Clyde at Broadwood in the league. Colin McMenamin scored two goals on his first start for the club, including a late winner to give the Black and Whites all three points.

And Kenny Deuchar also scored twice as Gretna eased into the second-round of the Challenge Cup with a comfortable 3-0 victory at Airdrie United.

Deuchar struck with a goal in each half, either side of a Steve Tosh strike as the Diamonds rarely threatened the Gretna goal at the Excelsior Stadium.

Hot-shot Colin McMenamin then hit a double on his full home debut in a 2-1 win over Ross County as Gretna maintained stayed at the top of Division One.

Brave Gretna took their league form into Europe but were eliminated from the UEFA Cup after a 2-2 draw with Derry City in the second-leg of the Second-Round Qualifying tie at the Brandywell Stadium.

But Rowan Alexander and his team could hold their heads high after a terrific first away performance in Europe in which they dominated for long periods and were unlucky not to score more goals.

The Gretna boss adopted an attacking 4-3-3 formation for the tie, with David Graham making his first start of the season up-front with Kenny Deuchar and James Grady.

The three frontmen combined well early on with James Grady chesting into the path of Graham only for his flashing drive to go past the post. Gretna went close again on 16 minutes when Kenny Deuchar got his head to a Stevie Tosh free-kick but he failed to trouble the Derry keeper.

However, Gretna's pressure paid off when a long ball from Main wasn't dealt with by Derry's defence and Darren Kelly's header fell to Graham. Without breaking stride, he took a touch and smashed a low 30-yard drive past keeper David Forde and into the net.

Gavin Skelton's ball over the top caught Derry square but the unlucky James Grady slipped in controlling his pass as it rolled frustratingly away from him.

Derry then levelled in the 37th minute as Kevin McHugh jinked down the wing and fed Stephen Farren in the box. Alan Main narrowed the angle, but Farren's shot deflected off his body and agonisingly in at the far post.

Gretna upped the tempo right from the start of the second half and Steve Tosh went close with a well-hit 20-yarder which sailed over, then a Deuchar effort was deflected wide.

But Derry went in front with 20 minutes to go as a corner went through a forest of legs and Ken Oman poked in. It was a body blow but Gretna kept on plugging away and were rewarded seven minutes later with the leveller.

Ryan Baldacchino, on as a 57th minute substitute for Mark Birch, was making rare appearance since suffering his knee-injury the previous January. And the winger marked his comeback with a goal, tucking the rebound into the net after Forde saved brilliantly to deny Kenny Deuchar.

Gretna continued to press but the home side secured a draw which took them comfortably through to the First Round of the competition 7-3 on aggregate.

"We showed great spirit and I'm delighted with the boys. They have done remarkably well and should get a pat on the back," said manager Alexander.

'We got our pride back and that's what we came here to do. It really wasn't about us trying to win the tie but showing we were a much better team than the first leg. It was a fantastic experience for everyone at the club and I was obviously happy with the performance tonight."

Derry boss Steven Kenny admitted: "At 1-0 down anything was possible and we had to get our act together and retain our composure. They were throwing the kitchen sink at us, using a long, direct style which is not normally their style because they are a good footballing side."

The European adventure was over but Gretna didn't have time to linger on it as they jetted home straight after the game for the important first-ever derby clash with Queen of the South at Palmerston and Colin McMenamin scored a double against his home-town team as Gretna secured a comfortable 3-0 victory as they kept at the top of the Division One table. The in-form striker, who hadn't signed in time to register for the European clashes, took his tally this season to six goals in four starts as Gretna stayed at the top of the First Division table.

Rowan Alexander was returning to the club which he once played for and managed and was delighted with the win.

"Our three strikers did remarkably well and they won the game for us today. They linked-up well together and we knew they would cause the opposition problems. Colin is hitting a rich vein of form just now and he gives us that cutting edge," he said.

"The atmosphere was fantastic and it shows you how far we've come when five-and-a half thousand turn up. I knew the welcome I'd get. Sometimes it's part of football. I had three successful years here and it's great to come back with another successful team I've built. They've gone out and shown a little bit of class today."

McMenamin replaced the suspended Kenny Deuchar, with Chris Innes, Allan Jenkins and John O'Neil also restored to the side.

Queens created the first chances when Sean O'Connor twice came close in the first five minutes as both sides looked to settle any early nerves. However, the home side were dealt a blow after 18 minutes when Graeme Weir was forced off with a fractured cheekbone to be replaced by Andy Thomson.

Cheered on by a fantastic 1,500 travelling fans, Gretna started to come into the game and Davie Graham was first to test Queens keeper Colin Scott, before a clever turn and shot by Colin McMenamin flew narrowly over the bar.

The pacy strikeforce of Graham, Grady and McMenamin caused the home defence problems and McMenamin had a great chance on 37 minutes, but he failed to connect properly with a John O'Neil cross. But two minutes later the striker latched on to a cut back from David Graham and jinked past two defenders before rounding Queens keeper Colin Scott and passing the ball into the empty net.

On the stroke of half-time Scott McKenzie gave away a free-kick on the edge of the box after a foul on James Grady. Danny Grainger stepped up and fired a superb shot into the bottom left-hand corner of the net past a despairing Colin Scott. The home side responded well and a great reflex save from Alan Main denied substitute Andy Thomson with the last kick of the first-half.

Gretna resumed after the break intent on adding to their tally with Skelton, Jenkins and Graham going close for the visitors. The Doonhamers afternoon got worse when striker Sean O'Connor was stretchered off after an hour with a suspected broken ankle.

Rowan Alexander's side continued to dominate and only a superb double save from Colin Scott denied Davie Graham from making it 3-0. Graham was again involved, this time combining well with McMenamin to set up Gavin Skelton but his shot was comfortably dealt with by Scott.

With two minutes remaining McMenamin scored his sixth of the season and wrapped up the points for the Black and Whites. Allan Jenkins rasping drive from 25 yards was parried by Queens keeper Colin Scott and the Dumfries-born striker headed home the rebound.

It was young Penrith-born defender Danny Grainger's first senior goal and he admitted it was a dream come true to see the ball hitting the back of the net.

"Scoring at Queens was the best thing I've had since I started playing in the first team," said Danny.

"It's always good to keep a clean sheet as a defender, but if you can get on the scoresheet as well it's even better. To score against Queen of the South, especially as I was there when I was younger, was just a great feeling."

"The lads were all pleased for me and it's good going into a team as young player as the lads all look after you well. When I scored everyone was happy for me, as I was for myself so it was good, especially in a local derby," he said.

Battling Derry were unlucky to go out of the UEFA Cup in the first round proper as they drew 0-0 with French giants Paris St. Germain at the Brandywell but went down 2-0 in Paris in the second leg.

By the New Year Gretna were 12 points clear at the top of the table and looked to be heading for the Scottish Premier League - the first club to go up through the Scottish Divisions in consecutive seasons - and ready to write another chapter in the story of the amazing little club from the small Border town famous for runaway marriages.

Steve Skinner nets against Clyde in the Cup (Top)

Gretna celebrate another goal. (Below)

Steve Tosh's spectacular overhead kick crashes in off the post to clinch the Division Three title. (Top)

Division Three Champions. (Below)

Division Two Champions. (Top)

Ryan McGuffie scores in the Scottish Cup Final. (Below)

So near yet so far...Gretna applaud winners Hearts. (Top)
Ryan McGuffie smashes in against Derry…..Gretna's
first ever goal in Europe. (Below)

Acknowledgements

Some of the reports inside first appeared in newspapers the News of the World, the News & Star and the Annandale Observer as well as the club's matchday programme.

The compilation of this book would not have been possible without the huge contributions of Alan Watson and Keith Melvin who wrote away match reports.

Cover and pictures used throughout by Alan Watson. Cover design by Keith Melvin.

To the players, management, officials and staff of Gretna FC who dared to dream - and pulled it off.

Brooks and Craig who made the dream a reality.

Look out for an official club history from 1986 to 2006 to come soon by Alan Watson.

Printed in the United Kingdom
by Lightning Source UK Ltd.
130057UK00001B/96/A

9 781846 855948